MEDITATION
AS A
WAY OF LIFE

MEDITATION AS A WAY OF LIFE

PHILOSOPHY AND PRACTICE

ROOTED IN THE TEACHINGS
OF PARAMAHANSA YOGANANDA

ALAN L. PRITZ

This publication has been generously supported by
The Kern Foundation

QUEST
BOOKS

Theosophical Publishing House
Wheaton, Illinois * Chennai, India

Quest Books
Theosophical Publishing House
PO Box 270
Wheaton, IL 60187-0270

www.questbooks.net

Cover image: Christian Keller/Thinkstock
Cover design by Mary Ann Smith
Illustrations by Randy Sehutt
Typesetting by DataPage, Inc.

Library of Congress Cataloging-in-Publication Data

Pritz, Alan L.
    Meditation as a way of life: philosophy and practice rooted in the teachings of Paramahansa Yogananda / Alan L. Pritz.
        pages   cm
Includes index.
ISBN 978-0-8356-0928-9
1. Meditation. 2. Yogananda, Paramahansa, 1893–1952. I. Title.
BL627.P74 2014
294.5'435—dc23   2014010444

5 4 3 2 1 * 14 15 16 17 18 19 20

Printed in the United States of America

~ In loving memory of Benjamin and Louise Pritz ~
I miss you.

Contents

Preface

The unfolding of every life is mysterious and often whimsical. Mine is no different. It has been a curious, often humorous, journey involving the study and application of spirituality within the context of a healing, teaching, writing, consulting, coaching, and interfaith ministerial career. *Meditation as a Way of Life*, an informal sequel to my *Pocket Guide to Meditation*, renders my acquired knowledge in a down-to-earth way to help people create a lifestyle grounded in spiritual disciplines and a meditative practice that is effective regardless of religious affiliation and is applicable to all faiths. The methods involved and the principles governing them are presented through the lens of my perspective, which is based on teachings of the modern spiritual master Paramahansa Yogananda that truth is universal and that one's relationship with God is enhanced through scientific meditation. Anyone, anywhere, can benefit by this content, confident that it is not based on belief or opinion, but on time-tested spiritual tenets.

Authority in any field, spiritual or mundane, stems from experience and related understanding. While involvement is no measure of wisdom, this book results from over forty years of committed participation in mind-body disciplines and immersion in meditative practices originating from an authentic spiritual tradition.

For those unfamiliar with meditation, it is not, as some modern expressions would depict it, a method to enhance health, boost creativity, or reduce stress. Those may be by-products of meditation, but they are not what meditation is about. This book presents meditation from a classical yogic perspective, as a discipline that involves mastering life force and consciousness to reunite the individual soul with Infinite Spirit. Meditation is founded on a worldview that ascribes to life a profound spiritual purpose and chronicles the soul's descent from Spirit into embodiment and its ultimate goal of reuniting with the Divine. The metaphysical (beyond the physical) principles related to meditation have been refined from thousands of years of inner pursuits and realizations about subtle realities. These matters transcend ideological differences, not by discounting diverse faith systems, but by revealing common esoteric threads and the spiritual harmony that unites them. Present in all valid religions is an underlying truth that serves as the basis upon which claims of universality arise. That truth is the foundation upon which this book is built.

The meditative practice and guidelines for spiritual living taught by Paramahansa Yogananda and presented here derive from cosmic laws that, unlike variable beliefs, doctrines, and dogma, which may shift individually or from creed to creed, are rooted in immutable verities relevant to all people regardless of culture, era, or worship preference. As has long been said, the sun shines equally on all. So, too, the tenets of Spirit operate without regard for religion, caste, color, gender, race, age, or other forms of human differentiation. Putting such principles into practice will only enrich one's relationship with the Divine. Readers are free to remain healthfully skeptical about any challenging topic, incorporating what rings true and deferring judgment on what seems questionable. This approach is prudent and self-honoring. Yet, discounting what is presented here merely because it seems unfamiliar may be rash. Until a critical mass of inner experience is acquired, the limitations of intellect often get in the way of subtle understanding. The best way to approach this material is with a receptive heart and an open mind.

Read, learn, and apply; the results will speak for themselves. "Doubt or no doubt, restless or calm, result or no result, keep meditating daily; but try to increase the depth of it, and you will get results. . . . After the negative state of silencing the mind is reached, meditation gives positive conscious contact with God as ever new joy, light and the cosmic sound of Aum."[1]

1

The Journey of Awakening

I f you are familiar with children, you can appreciate how their tenacious "Why, why?" questions can be challenging. Yet who can blame them for their questions: they live in the world and want to make sense of it. Natural inquiries often become more articulate or profound with age but, despite the polish of mature intellects, remain focused on basic meaning-of-life issues.

The quest to grasp why we are here represents a primal human need to solve the mystery of existence. Probing for answers has fostered philosophical and religious thought, yet despite extensive reflection the search continues. The unfolding tableau of theoretical physics, near-death phenomena, and past-life research has only intensified our pursuits. As knowledge of the outer universe expands, so does awareness of our inner nature. In some instances the line between physics and metaphysics resembles an ideological spectrum more than separate fields of inquiry.

In the television miniseries *Broken Trail*, the aging cowboy played by Robert Duvall reflects, "We are all travelers in this world. From the sweet grass to the packing house, birth till death, we travel between the eternities."[1] Eventually, everyone entertains questions about existence and feels compelled to explore life's meaning. When people do that, they begin a journey toward awakening. Just as seeds planted in fertile soil inexorably grow toward the light, we are evolutionarily called from an automatic-pilot existence toward one of spiritual awareness. Some come to this readily through an affinity for philosophy, religion, or natural wonder. Others seek relief from hardship through esoteric or religious study. By midlife, our stable routines often become haunted by issues of mortality and awareness that outer accomplishments are not necessarily the benchmarks of a life well lived.

Despite such prompts, a key question arises: why is there any evolutionary compulsion in the direction of self-inquiry? The answer is a bold but defensible statement: We are hardwired to seek connection with our Source. Consider that everyone is fundamentally motivated by a drive for fulfillment. Each of us has a conscious or unconscious desire to be happy, regardless of how that manifests individually. Epitomized for some as a spouse or family, for others it is a job, house, car, income, or power. Yet life repeatedly teaches—usually dramatically—that seeking happiness externally is a recipe for disappointment. Satisfaction arising from outer causes does exist, at least temporarily, but upon reflection it is clear that happiness is not a fundamental component of things (or people) per se but arises from our reactions to them. These reactions reflect a capacity to access a preexisting inner joy that reveals itself when tapped by external circumstances. If joy were an ingredient of externals, it would engender universal responses rather than subjective ones. For example, when splashed with water we all get wet; that is objective and universal. Our reaction to getting splashed, however, be it glee or annoyance, is subjective and is not a quality of the water itself. Thus, the sense of fulfillment we get from people or things is a relative one subject to our reactions. This temporary sense of fulfillment is prone to innumerable variables that may shift unpredictably. Enduring relationships are complexities in and of themselves and worthy of the effort, but they too must be guided by wisdom in order to last. The bold truth is that nothing outside us produces or sustains lasting joy. Even those who allegedly have it all eventually experience emptiness if their measures of life satisfaction are hung on temporal rungs. Joy is part of our inner domain and must be reaped from its interior source to ensure sustainability.

Understandably, we want whatever happiness we have to stay. When it does not, we blame a laundry list of culprits—spouses, jobs, money—for being inadequate and complicating our lives. But existential dilemmas such as these are never fully attributable to outside factors; they arise largely within us from regions composing our essential core. When we are disconnected from this essence and what it provides, external affairs gain power over our peace of mind. Negative mental states spawn diverse forms of physical or emotional distress, but all fundamentally manifest spiritual malaise. Such distress compels us to corrective actions, which inevitably include meaning-of-life reflection. Yet, again, why are we flung into this messy dynamic? Because we are esoterically confused creatures of paradox. Incarnate physically, we are not, as the singer Madonna suggests, material beings living in a material world. That is a delusion many succumb to and inevitably suffer from. The famed Jesuit Teilhard de Chardin rightly declared, "We are not human beings having a spiritual experience. We are spiritual beings having a human experience."[2] His assertion testifies to a deep reality. Our essence, that which imbues us with consciousness, call it soul or Spirit, hails from that which created it. Since we are a component of the Divine, our souls necessarily seek completion through reuniting with it, and that compels us accordingly. Wholeness or fulfillment, therefore, can never be gotten from temporal means, but solely by returning to our source.

Why is this fundamental principle not more obvious? Why do we consistently rely on sensory or material gratification to make us feel complete and repeatedly wind up in pitiful straits? That is because of the esoteric paradox. Soul cravings are blurred by the body containers in which they are housed, and, complicating matters further, the world supports this misperception. Our complex psychophysical constitutions are such that spiritual drives get muddied when routed through body/mind channels that link satisfaction with sensory stimuli. We are motivated by various impulses, only to find that many of them arise from, and distort, soul-based longings. It is a perverse system, certainly a recipe for heartache, but there it is. Take love for example. We want love and go to great lengths to acquire it, but why? On one level it makes us feel good, complete, or connected to something bigger than ourselves.

Unfortunately, this search for love often leads us to "all the wrong places." The truth is that we want love because it, too, is part of our spiritual constitution. Our essence is love, and, like moths drawn to light, we crave it. Love in turn produces joy; thus the soul fundamentally yearns for love and joy because they compose the nature of Spirit, with which we seek alignment. Viewing the quest for love and joy through this lens shifts life perspectives considerably.

Human love and relationships are not to be dismissed, but the compulsions for each are clearly not as simple as they seem. They are rooted in soul-based spiritual drives that go beyond the temporal to the eternal, which is why spiritual giants—Jesus, Krishna, and Buddha to name but three—uniformly warned against putting stock in the world. It will not deliver what the soul craves.

According to Christian tradition as expressed by John in his First Epistle, this sentiment is succinctly presented as: "Love not the world, neither the things that are in the world. If any man love the world, the love of the Father is not in him. For all that is in the world, the lust of the flesh, and the lust of the eyes, and the pride of life, is not of the Father, but is of the world. And the world passeth away, and the lust thereof: but he that doeth the will of God abideth for ever."[3]

Krishna similarly exorts spiritual aspirants to keep singularly focused on the divine in all circumstances: "But whereso any doeth all his deeds, renouncing self for Me, full of Me, fixed to serve only the Highest, night and day musing on Me—him will I swiftly lift forth from life's ocean of distress and death whose soul clings fast to Me. Cling thou to Me! Clasp Me with heart and mind! So shalt thou dwell surely with Me on high."[4]

And Buddha preached Four Noble Truths and the Eightfold Path, directing people away from wrong thinking, desire, and the suffering they produce because he sought their greatest good, a spiritual potential not realized through temporal fixation or endeavors.

All spiritual masters teach that lasting happiness cannot be gained from transient worldly means. Refuge in the eternal is the only way to enduring fulfillment.

On the plus side, earthly disillusionment is a magnificent, rather crafty nudge toward spiritual inquiry and reconciliation. We need not become anything, but merely recollect what we already are: Spirit. Consider legendary figures like Francis of Assisi, Ramana Maharshi, Moses, Mohammed, or the Buddha. Each had relatively ordinary lives until extraordinary events transpired. Through grace and dedication to higher pursuits, they attained levels of illumination we all innately seek. They also demonstrated that their realizations are not for a select few but are available to all. As gold covered by mud nevertheless remains gold, once the grime of spiritual debris is removed our spiritual essence is revealed. Again, we need not become anything, but merely reconnect with what we already are: Spirit. We are all soul waves bobbing on a sea of Spirit. The ocean of Spirit knows it has created these waves, yet the waves must recall that they are of the ocean. Those willing to plumb the depths of consciousness will, eventually, come to this realization.

Sensory pleasures and material acquisition can never be our ultimate goals; they simply do not provide what the soul needs. Since we are souls only temporarily encased in bodies, our requirements for fulfillment must be aligned with our source. This truth is what prompts us to self-discovery through the vicissitudes of life. Once these matters are embraced, the journey of awakening begins and inexorably leads us to completion in Spirit. Although worldly influences can temporarily derail us from the inner journey, those ready to undertake it will find the journey beneficial. Just as sparks of self-inquiry may be fanned into flames of wisdom, using the methods of meditation provided herein will help seekers walk the transformative path and harvest the fruits of Spirit latent within.

My Tale

Amusingly, my inner journey began when I was quite young and was watching a television Western. There was little to recommend most cowboy plots: heroes, villains, and ladies in distress—archetypal elements set amid horses, whiskey, and tumbleweed. This particular show, a dimly recalled episode of some sort, but not to be confused with the later TV series called *Kung Fu*, was unique because it featured two samurai warriors out West. Predictably, whenever these men passed through frontier towns local rowdies wanted to fight. The samurai inevitably dispatched them with martial-art skills and continued on, leaving sore wranglers in their wake. Seeing those two fight—victoriously yet dispassionately—converted my childish emulation of the sword-fighting hero Zorro into something more exotic. Karate-like attacks on anything that moved became the norm, and eventually my parents enrolled me in martial arts training, on the condition that I lay off the dog.

Tales of my prowess would be fabricated: I was not Bruce Lee. I was a dedicated but unremarkable martial arts student who simply persisted. This anecdote of my brown-belt test offers an accurate, if humbling, perspective.

In the martial arts world, the brown-belt test is a serious rite of passage from clumsy beginner to relatively advanced student. Until this point, the idea of being a black belt inhabited a quasi-mythic, unobtainable domain. Suddenly it was within reach.

As with most martial arts exams, testing is open to the public. Guests gather, classmates flit about self-importantly, teachers coalesce into judging panels, and you try to look devastating. Since I was a timid sort, this test was a nerve-racking event I had dreaded for months. Test day came, and I arrived anxious and distracted. En route to the locker room I noticed my car keys were missing, not a good thing given my strained disposition. In near panic, I retraced my steps outside and, with mixed relief, saw my car was safe and . . . still running. No more need be said.

As for the test, I passed. Ten years later found me a black belt in two systems, one in my primary Chinese style and another in a Korean tradition. In fact, I excelled as one of a group of advanced students and was promoted to the rank of sifu, or teacher—proof that even mediocre ability could be transformed by hard work and commitment.

This era was noteworthy for cultivating in me a healthy body and a broad, receptive mind. When not training or teaching, I avidly read about mysticism to gain insight into nonordinary laws and subtle realities. My metaphysical curiosity grew beyond what was accessible in the martial domain, so I turned toward yoga, meditation in particular. Such pursuits were not widely popular back then where I lived, so it was hard knowing how to proceed. Unlike the biblical Job, who was relentlessly pummeled by divine tests, my knowledge-gathering process was akin to Monty Python's search for the Holy Grail. The Divine allowed me free rein for comedic value. As mentioned, I knew what I wanted—meditation training—but knew not how to get it. Consequently, my journey lurched forward inelegantly. In fact, while experimenting with anything that could propel me forward, I fell under the narrative spell of a book about yogic adepts. In emulative fashion I decided to test my mettle by practicing austerities, an inconceivably foolish idea without proper guidance. One evening I entered a sauna, assumed a meditative pose, and settled in to conquer heat sensitivity. As time passed, I no longer felt hot and exalted in this seeming first triumph over the flesh. The truth was less glamorous. Lack of sensation came not from mystical ability but from sweat: the body's cooling system was simply doing its job. Several hours later my rump felt uncommonly tender. A subsequent, discreet exam revealed an enormous blister formed in a delicate area, proof that, despite my mental aspirations toward transcendence, my nether regions failed to oblige!

Offbeat experiences aside, mysticism captivated me. Sages of all faiths shared transcendental insights that common religionists lacked. Gazing beyond the bounds of ritualized dogma, they spoke authoritatively of principles that guided the destinies of people and planets. I was passionate to learn about this area, as it revealed an underlying order and intelligent purpose behind the apparent chaos of creation. Chief among influential books was *Autobiography of a Yogi* by Paramahansa Yogananda. Curiously, my first response to this book was to feel slightly disconcerted: I could not tell by the cover photo if the author was male or female. I later learned that such androgyny reflected perfect masculine/feminine balance and was reminded not to judge books, or people, by appearances. After cracking the book open, I was enthralled. The recounting of this master's life touched me profoundly. Being ready for its message and in a position to act upon it, I put my belongings into storage and went to a mountain retreat in California, where I could obtain the meditation and spiritual training I yearned for.

Understand that spirituality is neither a code word for impracticality nor an excuse for irresponsibility. Radical actions like mine are not recommended per se; they can create more difficulty than they are worth. My situation, however, was such that this step felt right. Being single, without debt, and seven years into the same job, I needed a vital redirection for my life. Additional academics or another job simply were not the answer. For months I had experienced a strange pull westward. This did not make sense at the time since I was not prone to such phenomena, but I now recognize it as inner guidance. Fortunately, I was able to heed that call, studied with an accomplished teacher, and gained the tools for my life's work. And a life's work it is, because, unlike ordinary graduate pursuits that are mostly scholastic, meditative competency is assessed by direct realization. Seeds of insight yield the fruits of wisdom only after years of disciplined practice and cultivation.

Given this framework, I advise readers to heed circumstances that feel significant. Curiously random events may actually hint at important steps on one's sojourn. For instance, a former student once shared how she had been browsing for inner growth books when *Autobiography of a Yogi* virtually leapt off a shelf at her. She subsequently heard of my kindred meditation trainings and enrolled in a class. Her friends found this synchronicity unnerving; I consider it natural. As the saying goes, "When the student is ready, the teacher will appear." The scenario had naught to do with me, other than I was available as a teacher when the evolutionary warp in her karma enabled her to act upon her spiritual curiosity. It merely reflected patterns set to promote those ready to step onto higher soul terrain. A biblically similar expression is, "Ask, and it shall be given you; seek, and ye shall find; knock, and it shall be opened unto you."[5] Guidance is always available, although sometimes it is whimsically rendered. Here is an example:

On the cusp of leaving for California, I was emotionally conflicted. Abandoning the familiar to pursue meditation training was a leap of faith, especially with no job or friends to buffer the experience. Swinging between joy, sadness, and doubt, I opted to drown my woes in Chinese food. I coaxed a neighbor to join me for dinner, and table talk inevitably turned to imminent concerns: "Should I go or not?" Our conversation resolved nothing, yet after the bill arrived and fortune cookies with it, I opened mine and laughed, for, of all possible things, it said, "Yes, go ahead with confidence!" Ancient oracles might have used sacred rituals to interpret divine will, but evidently Spirit chose a more comedic delivery system with me.

Beneath the obvious humor is a significant spiritual lesson: Do not get derailed by doubt. Change is tough, and people often prefer the known over the unknown, even when it hurts. Despite wanting improvement, good intentions are frequently derailed by weak resolve. Why? On one level, bad habits are simply hard to break. On a grander scale, creation contains positive and negative forces that affect us all. Where there is light, there is also darkness. There is hard and soft, good and bad, yin and yang. All coexist; none abides without the other. Newton's third law of motion describes this phenomenon as, "For every action, there is an equal and opposite reaction."[6] Metaphysically, as we pursue positive directions, oppositional inclinations often get activated. They can manifest in every aspect of life. Consider how friends invite you over for homemade pasta just after you start a diet. In spiritual matters, this curious phenomenon manifests when high-minded aspirations trigger sabotaging tendencies or counterparts. For example, self-discipline may attract temptation; faith may attract doubt; forgiveness may attract grudges.

Consider the classic cartoon of a devil sitting on one shoulder while an angel perches on the other. Both whisper in your ears to influence you, yet you must choose the correct counsel. Movement toward light may awaken the shadow, but that is okay. One does not get strong by wrestling babies, and you will not be abandoned. Persistence in right resolve attracts supportive aid. Negative forces are effective only when granted consent. If defeatist voices arise within, conquer them through wisdom. Impersonal demons are but metaphysical pests intent on promoting failure. Swat them away and forge ahead with confidence.

Returning to my narrative, after overcoming my predeparture woes, a joyous sense of adventure arose that lasted through my westward trek. Then, a second wave of resistance struck. Arriving at the California retreat, I paused, immobilized before its isolated roadway, thinking, "What the blazes am I doing?" Worse, I could virtually hear my older brother trumpeting with laughter. My family was not overly fond of my ashram investigation, and, although I stayed the course, over the next six months my brother regularly called the communal-retreat phone asking whoever answered if he could speak with "the Mahatma," his code name for me. Bless older brothers. Having little choice, I took his jibes in stride, figuring they must be part of my unscripted training.

At the onset of my ashram adventure, I was not only stricken with residual cold feet but, in addition, my car died. Having fulfilled its transcontinental contract, it took a sabbatical that left me stranded and unable to contemplate diversions until needed repairs were made. Accordingly, I stiffened my resolve to enjoy myself and learn what I could. After all, I had pursued this course, not vice versa. The initial routines were so novel that I did not miss anything from my prior life. Two weeks later, however, found me descending into haloed stir-craziness. Hatha yoga, chanting, meditation, and philosophy were elevating; scenic vistas were pleasant company; and a healthy lifestyle was hardly torturous; but such sanctity grew wearisome. Without television, restaurants, or movies, I suffered from stimulus deprivation and craved an evening of something decidedly nondevotional. The nearest town was too far to reach by foot, so a kindred neophyte and I plotted a cure for our goody-two-shoes blues: pilfering organic grapefruit from the ashram larder. It was a lame diversion, but the forbidden fruit actually did taste exceptional!

As is often the case with thwarted desires, my deprivations proved remarkably insightful. In spite of myself I began to settle in and settle down. Lacking significant distractions, I became calmer and increasingly attuned to the mountain environment. Vistas became lovelier, and the peace churned from meditative routine became distinctly more pleasurable. I began having a delightful time. Once my car was repaired, though, I raced to town for the buzz of urban activity. Surprisingly, I found myself jarred by even minor amounts of stimulation. I realized that most people—including myself—are addicted to activity. Workaday lives are saturated with it, and holiday themes are often chosen for high-adrenaline adventure. Value is rarely placed on simply *being*, and cultivating calmness does not factor into most people's lives. This is ironic because resting the nerves enhances sensory perception and the capacity for enjoyment. For example, when we have been sick and holed up in a house for several days and then step outside after recovering, the world virtually sparkles. It has not changed; our quality of perception has. The lesson of my escape-to-town adventure was that meditation interiorizes awareness and refines its external capacity. Needless to say, I embraced the remaining retreat time with increased enthusiasm and receptivity to events around and within me. When it was time for me to move on, I did so as a far more integrated and conscious person.

The journey of awakening does not require a somber attitude, excessive piety, drama, or anything else beyond sincerity and showing up. The journey is for anyone ready to take it and willing to pay the coin of self-effort. Let the truth as you understand it continue to guide you. Stay open, enjoy whatever transpires, and let the process unfold naturally.

2

Terms and Concepts

Much can be said about the distinctions between religion and spirituality and, in fact, will be, in the appendix. I generally deem spirituality as nondenominational and ideally suited for inner awakening: It promotes direct experience of the holy and methods to achieve it. Adding to this mix are central concepts of God, Self-realization, truth, the dream fabric of reality, the nature of creation, and soul struggle that need to be addressed in the context of this book to help move the process of spiritual development forward in a meaningful way. By that I mean that the subjects involved should be intellectually understandable as well as personally perceivable. In short, there is a reasoned basis for why each step on the spiritual path, meditation in particular, is undertaken. It helps truth seekers maintain proper perspective and fortifies their resolve when these steps and related paradigms are known. Each subject merits extensive elaboration, but my explanations will be kept comprehensively succinct. Although the ideas are rooted in the teachings of my lineage and Vedic tradition, the material is relevant for all persons since the underlying truths are universal in nature.

GOD

What is God? It seems almost comical to provide an answer to such a question, but without doing so all religionists and spiritual people are effectively dedicating their hearts, minds, and souls to something without knowing what it is. Many of us do just that! We are comfortable with ascribing to the transcendent a degree of the unfathomable that insulates us from rational scrutiny. Fortunately, there are some who have experienced the Divine directly and have been able to accurately ascribe to it features and qualities that satisfy the mind of humankind. To say that God is a loving, transcendent, immanent, omnipresent, omniscient, omnipotent Spirit is well and good, but such concepts do little to justify a need for God. And without that need, attention to God becomes more an honoring of religious obligation than a daily practical necessity. To appreciate the unfathomable, we must first highlight the qualities that make it most evident to us, and these are two primal factors: force and intelligence. Force—or power—and the intelligence governing it are the universal matrix. Lacking force, nothing in nature can function. Without intelligence, the universe cannot be harmoniously organized. Intelligence must guide and control the myriad interactions of creation—its manifestation, preservation, dissolution—lest it fail to coalesce and operate effectively. Random chance is not a viable hypothesis when considering the inconceivable intricacy required to create life or sustain a balanced universe. Christian and Hindu holy texts concur:

> I am Alpha and Omega, the beginning and the ending, saith the Lord, which is, and which was, and which is to come, the Almighty.[1]

> I am death that carries off all, and the origin of things that are to be. . . . All beings pass into My primordial nature at the end of a world-eon; and I send them forth again at the beginning of a new world-eon.[2]

Since intelligence guides the constitution of matter and force vivifies it, one working definition of God might be "that invisible factory of intelligence that creates, gives birth to, and harmoniously develops all manifested things" or the "supreme intelligence (or consciousness) that governs everything."[3] We may accept the idea of an infinitely intelligent force, but even that is not fully satisfying. At some level we all crave immortality. This desire reflects the soul's innate awareness of its eternal nature. By similar measure, the soul also quietly informs us of its native state of full awareness and perpetual joy, since the idea of perpetual unconsciousness or misery is anathema to us. From this we may ascribe to God a more complete description as the supreme, ever newly conscious, existent, and blissful intelligent force that creates and guides all creation.

When Spirit is depicted as such, it behooves us to develop an attunement with it, since guidance by a supreme consciousness is undeniably better than guidance from our lesser human minds. Similarly, aligning with the Divine becomes imminently practical when God is perceived as ever newly conscious, existent, blissful, and the source of perpetual happiness. A dedicated relationship with God subsequently forms the basis for a happy, insightful, and successful life, not to mention a spiritually elevating one. Real spiritual savants have not been failed materialists. They have been able to tap and operate the laws underlying creation for optimal spiritual and material success. The following scenario is an example of this:

> A friend of mine said I was all right as a spiritual man, but that I could not succeed in business. I replied, "I am going to make five thousand dollars in business for you, within two weeks." He said, "You will have to show me. I am from Missouri." I did not rush to invest money on unwise things. I used concentration, disengaged my mind of all disturbances, and focused my attention on one thing. (Most of us have the searchlight of our attention turned outside all the time instead of inside—we should turn the searchlight of the mind on the divine source. Every change in business, every change in the planetary system, in the physical system—everything is recorded there. We are living on one side of the universe; the other side is more tangible than this side.) So I touched that source. Ordinarily men do not concentrate—the mind is restless, and

the restless mind jumps at conclusions and races for something that does not belong to it. You must obey the law. Remember, concentrate and then ask Divine Power. Thus, as soon as I contacted that source, there were shown to me lots of houses. But I did not sit quietly in my room and say, "The Heavenly Father will open the ceiling and drop five thousand dollars in my lap," because I have favored Him with a fervent prayer. I bought the Sunday papers and looked at real estate advertisements. I picked out a few houses, and told my friend to invest his money in them. He said, "Everything seems pretty shaky," and I said, "Never mind, doubting Thomas, don't try to spoil success by your doubts." In two weeks there was a real estate boom and prices of houses went way up high. He sold the houses and had a clear profit of five thousand dollars. I showed him that the power of God or mind works wherever we apply it with faith.[4]

Ultimately, accurate knowledge of God cannot be gained by the human intellect because it is limited and provides only partial, indirect information. God must be realized through the soul's unerring and inherent capacity to discern truth directly, without the intermediary aid of the senses. This refined skill enabling direct discernment of truth is known as intuition. Meditation is the principal means of cultivating intuition and, consequently, unfettered joy and wisdom.

SELF-REALIZATION

Self-realization means insight into one's true Self, the soul, not ego personality. According to Yogananda, Self-realization is "the knowing—in body, mind, and soul—that we are one with the omnipresence of God; that we do not have to pray that it come to us, that we are not merely near it at all times, but that God's omnipresence is our omnipresence;

that we are just as much a part of Him now as we ever will be. All we have to do is improve our knowing."[5] The soul is an eternal unit of the unchanging Divine that is incarnate in human form and is indistinguishable from God itself. God is the source from which all souls come, the substance out of which all souls are made, and the abode to which all souls finally return. Spiritually speaking, reuniting with the Absolute is the principal goal of existence and can be attained by practices that culminate in Self-realization. As explained by the venerable saint Ramana Maharshi, "Happiness is inherent in man and is not due to external causes. One must realize himself in order to experience his unalloyed happiness."[6] In the term *Self-realization*, *realization* is used instead of *knowledge* because spiritual awakening is experiential, not intellectual. Knowledge implies duality—a separation of knower from the known. Realization, on the other hand, is that experience in which the knower is directly identified with the known, and consequently no separateness exists. Knowledge is relative and incomplete because of its inherent duality; realization is absolute because there is no relativity in complete unity.

TRUTH

Truth is the unwavering fabric of existence that we can realize or express but not create. Seeing only creation's dualistic nature, people often consider truth to be a relative matter that can accommodate variable life conditions. They fail to cognize it as an absolute condition. Yet, eternal truth, referred to in both the Buddhist and Hindu traditions as dharma, is just that: exact correspondence with supreme reality. It underlies, imbues, and sustains creation yet transcends readily perceivable experience. It is the essence of wisdom and a liberating goal: "And ye shall know the truth, and the truth shall make you free."[7] Without truth there would be no basis for ethical standards, philosophical inquiry, or science—all of which strive to discern the laws of being and live in harmonious accord with them. In a spiritual context, truth affirms our intrinsic soul nature and the primary purpose of existence: to overcome the delusion of separation from Spirit and to regain conscious unity with the Divine.

THE DREAM FABRIC OF REALITY

At a lecture I once gave on "Creating Inner Peace during Turbulent Times," I told the audience of lively and intellectually curious retired nuns that what we experience as creation is actually the condensed "thought stuff" of Spirit, a vivid cosmic manifestation of extremely subtle vibrations. Its seemingly solid reality disappears when we awaken in divine consciousness. Knowing this comment could be seen as trivializing the pain and suffering everyone periodically endures, I shared a vision of comfort and consolation that my master had during WWI:

> One day I entered a cinema house to view a newsreel of the European battlefields. The First World War was still being waged in the West; the newsreel presented the carnage with such realism that I left the theater with a troubled heart.
>
> "Lord," I prayed, "why dost Thou permit such suffering?"
>
> To my intense surprise, an instant answer came in the form of a vision of the actual European battlefields. The scenes, filled with the dead and dying, far surpassed in ferocity any representation of the newsreel.
>
> "Look intently!" A gentle Voice spoke to my inner consciousness. "You will see that these scenes now being enacted in France are nothing but a play of chiaroscuro. They are the cosmic motion picture, as real and as unreal as the theater newsreel you have just seen—a play within a play."

My heart was still not comforted. The Divine Voice went on: "Creation is light and shadow both, else no picture is possible. The good and evil of *maya* must ever alternate in supremacy. If joy were ceaseless here in this world, would man ever desire another? Without suffering, he scarcely cares to recall that he has forsaken his eternal home. Pain is a prod to remembrance. The way of escape is through wisdom. The tragedy of death is unreal; those who shudder at it are like an ignorant actor who dies of fright on the stage when nothing more has been fired at him than a blank cartridge. My sons are children of light; they will not sleep forever in delusion."[8]

This story was not intended to minimize the impact of individual or collective trials, but to provide a fortifying perspective and solace. It is challenging to keep this world in correct context, yet spiritually imperative to do so. Right understanding does not lessen compassion, but provides the strength to face and pass life's inevitable trials without loss of inner equilibrium.

THE NATURE OF CREATION

Human Beings

As people may wear several layers of clothes, the incarnate soul—our essential being—wears three distinct "overcoats." The finest or most subtle one is called the causal or ideational body. It is made of thought and consists of thirty-five ideas that emanate from Spirit. In turn, it forms a substructure for two denser coverings, the astral body of light with nineteen energetic components and the physical body with sixteen chemical ingredients. These diversely vibrating bodies encase the soul in an integrated structure that comprises every human being.

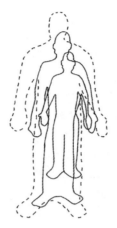

This model is part of classic Vedic teachings on gross and spiritual anatomy and is honored by esoteric mystery schools of many traditions. I can vouch for its authenticity, at least in part. A feat called astral projection involves separating the astral form from the physical body. It is commonly known as an out-of-body experience. Adepts say it requires skill to do consciously but occurs naturally during sleep. Without pretensions to being a mystical virtuoso, I have undergone this adventure multiple times. During the disembodied state, I have met other souls, traveled to mysterious regions, and hovered in deep space while being fully aware that I am out of my body. Ordinarily I do not mention such matters because they are difficult to verify and appeal mostly to those fascinated by spiritual phenomena. But they are true experiences.

Similar incidents are chronicled in a variety of books, a notable one being Dr. Raymond Moody's *Life After Life: The Investigation of a Phenomenon—Survival of Bodily Death*. Although some researchers argue that out-of-body states are just symptoms of oxygen deprivation to the brain, those who have had genuine astral experiences report being able to recall clearly otherwise unaccountable details. Hospital-setting scenarios of this type depict critically injured patients who die and rise above their bodies, then hear and see conversations that would ordinarily be beyond sensory range. After reentering the body and regaining consciousness, they report these experiences with vivid detail. While clearly unusual for most Westerners, such soul-journey phenomena are not unusual for many Eastern or indigenous belief systems. In fact, shamans in certain traditions routinely engage in purposeful astral projection as part of their tribal duties. Again, these themes are not new; they are merely not commonly taught in Abrahamic traditions. The truth remains that we are not simply physical beings. We are conscious sparks of omnipresent Spirit, souls that temporarily incarnate in physical form. The famed maxim of Descartes, "Cogito ergo sum—I think, therefore I am,"[9] is esoterically incorrect. It should be, "I am, therefore I think." Consciousness precedes thought and gives rise to form.

Transition at death to bodies of light is not mythic; it refers to the dropping of physical form and continuation in an astral body in an astral world. The astral and causal bodies surrounding the soul remain intact when the physical body falls away. Our fundamental existence never ends, for these subtle bodies perpetuate our manifestation on corresponding planes of consciousness. For example, the astral body keeps us engaged in the astral domain, the causal in its realm. Reincarnation refers to the perpetual and automatic process of incarnating physically until, by spiritual realization, we learn to overcome that which binds us to the material sphere: desire. Through increasing association with soul consciousness, we gradually shed identification with the physical, astral, and causal casings and eventually reunite with our source. This progression is a natural evolutionary process arising from realizing one's soul essence. Think of a bird born in captivity. When its cage doors are opened, it naturally stays in the cage—that is all it knows. Gradually it hops to the lip of the cage, flies outside in exploratory forays, and then returns to its perceived home. Eventually, instinct compels it to fly away forever and reclaim its birthright of limitless freedom. The same thing applies to us. As we gradually come to experience and identify with our infinite nature, the body becomes a place of confinement for the otherwise omnipresent soul. When we drop all bodily constraints, physical or subtle, and return as unhindered souls to our celestial home in Spirit, we consciously reclaim our eternal freedom in omnipresence.

The Universal Drama

In my tradition, which is fundamentally based on Vedism, the purpose of spiritual practice is linked to the nature of the universe. Everything is created due to the Divine's intention to share the bliss of its being. Since Spirit is absolute and singular, it manifested all things out of itself and fashioned an appearance of duality to imbue creation with relative diversity and autonomy. Regardless of its infinite variety, all existence is made of just one thing: Spirit. This phenomenon can be likened to ocean waves that arise from the sea and appear endlessly distinct, yet are fundamentally similar units of one source.

Humanity is uniquely crafted compared to the innumerable other manifestations in creation. The human body is made after the pattern of animals, yet embedded in the animal body/mind is a soul made after the pattern of God. Humanity has a spiritual anatomy able to foster realization of its derivation from, and essential unity with, God. Earth-directed souls are meant to experience the material plane in a state of blissful divine consciousness and then revert into Spirit. Unfortunately, an independent aspect of the creative force empowered to oversee the creative process—called Maya by Hindus, Mara by Buddhists, and Satan by Christians—chooses to oppose the divine plan. By fashioning primal subterfuges of delusion and desire, it lures souls from Spirit and perpetuates their status in embodied manifestation. Omnipotent God can remedy this situation easily but allows free will to remain, albeit imperfectly expressed, knowing divine love will inevitably attract all creation back to its source, Spirit. The purpose of spiritual practice in light of this perspective is to overcome the delusive illusion of separation from Spirit and reawaken in complete conscious unity with the Godhead. It is a microcosmic or personal response to a macrocosmic or universal situation.

SOUL STRUGGLE

The Fall of humanity scenario symbolically rendered in the Garden of Eden allegory depicts the God-persona or soul in humans striving to overcome its animal aspect in a battle between flesh and Spirit. And all this traces back to the oppositional force's creative malfeasance. The esoteric meaning of being cast out of Paradise, or "falling," is important on many subtle levels. It fundamentally refers to the descent of consciousness within humankind from a soul-based state of God-union (paradise) into alienation from God through identification with the physical body and subsequent fixation on physical reality. Perceiving only the material aspects of themselves and nature, people become confused and divorced from subtle spiritual awareness and the perception of God.

The Garden of Eden refers to the human body. The tree of life is the spine, with efferent and afferent nerves like branches of an inverted tree, having its roots located at the crown of the head. The fruits of the garden represent various sense faculties and related perceptions. The trees in the center of the garden refer to the different nervous systems, and the tree of the knowledge of good and evil pertains to the regenerative region and its fruit of sexual sensation/experience/indulgence. The serpent is the spirally ascending kundalini force (latent spiritual energy) located at the base of the spine. Adam and Eve signify the first humans. In the Garden of God-consciousness, the law is, "Of every tree of the garden you may freely eat [enjoy all sense faculties] but of the tree of the knowledge of good and evil [sexual expression] you shall not eat [indulge]; for in the day that you eat of it you shall surely die."[10] Modern readers do not readily appreciate this edict, as it apparently

23

warns against participating in what most consider inherently natural, loving, and procreative urges. Yet the esoteric premise, regardless of any disapprobation, is that prior to engaging in sexual activity, humans existed in a state of God-consciousness and were empowered to create by divine fiat; physical means were unnecessary. Eating of the tree of knowledge of good and evil, i.e., sex activity, brought their elevated consciousness down from a plane of unity to one of duality—good and evil—subsequently compromising the divine power heretofore exercised. This descent of consciousness into relativity is the Fall.

Elucidating further, in every individual there is said to be an Adam, a masculine component endowed with a preponderantly rational, analytic quality. Likewise, everyone also has an Eve, a feminine component equipped with a predominantly emotional or feeling principle. When the serpent, or kundalini, force ascends the spine, it stimulates the sexual nervous system, triggering a desire to engage in related behaviors. When the feminine feeling principle is confronted with this impulse, it tempts the masculine analytic principle to comply. Unless successfully resisted, the masculine rational quality succumbs. Once the original sexual experience occurred, the dual "knowledge of good and evil" replaced that of celestial unity, and immaculate creative abilities were reduced to those of physical effort, "working by the sweat of the brow." Being cast out of paradise, therefore, meant the descent of consciousness from the divine sphere to the relative sphere.

The law of reincarnation is another effect of the Fall, set in motion by the delusive force to extend periods of soul embodiment. The admonition "for in the day that you eat of it you shall surely die" implies that instead of reuniting with Spirit after an earthly stay, souls are compelled by the law of karma to repeatedly incarnate physically until all material desires are expunged. This law explains why the Buddha taught that desire is the root of all suffering; it blinds souls from perceiving their true spiritual essence and binds them to the wheel of reincarnation. As mentioned earlier, spiritual practices—meditation in particular—are linked to this creation drama as deliberate efforts to win release from cyclic rebirth. Souls attain final emancipation or salvation by realizing their true nature and then consciously reascend to unite with God.

Herein lies a metaphysical rendering of creation and the descent of humanity. The fall from divine unity into the sphere of duality is the stage upon which every soul must struggle to regain its inherent and ultimate freedom in Spirit. The soul-over-flesh struggle is so fundamental to the spiritual journey that it bears revisiting: The soul identified with the physical plane becomes swayed by sensory influences. Spiritual yearnings routed through the body confuse enjoyable nerve sensations manifesting as physical pleasure with the lasting, innate joy of Spirit. Thus deluded, the soul lingers in worldly infatuation until it realizes that the bliss it craves cannot be had by material means. Then it struggles to overcome the constraints of nature and attendant cycles of reincarnation to find lasting satisfaction in Spirit. Again, the soul's fall into delusion, its repentance, and its eventual return home is a universal tale. Many Eastern traditions describe this process as liberation. Christianity calls it salvation: "Him that overcometh will I make a pillar in the temple of my God, and he shall go no more out."[11] And Abrahamic traditions hide the archetype within the Prodigal Son parable. Here is an interpretive rendering:

There were two sons (souls) and their father (God). The younger son asked for and received his inheritance (divine independence and free will). Leaving home (oneness with Spirit), he traveled far and lost his wealth to dissolute living (fell prey to sense entanglements and body identification). Becoming subject to famine and the stinginess of others (karmic consequences of wrong actions), the son realized he would fare better at home (recognition of error). He went back to his father and, assuming he was unworthy of a son's status, asked to be accepted as a servant (repentance). Instead of a meager welcome, the father held a wonderful feast (divine compassion and forgiveness). Upon hearing this, the elder son grew angry, complaining that the father never treated him lavishly despite his obedient behavior. The father responded that his faithfulness had guaranteed constant access to his wealth (he was in perpetual at-one-ment with Spirit). The younger son, however, had been as if dead to him. He lost himself (fell from divine union) through folly (delusion), yet was found anew (returned to his true home in Spirit). As such, it was fitting to celebrate (forgive) the return (repentance and self-effort) of a dearly loved one from the grave of error (reincarnation cycles) to a righteous life (redemption and resurrection in Spirit).

This drama is everyone's drama, for we have all strayed. However, despite countless errors over innumerable lives, we must retain awareness of being eternal souls, not everlasting sinners. Sin is ignorance, a graft of inharmonious deed or thought that impedes recognizing our ever-perfect Self. Affirmation of sinner status is a metaphysical error, for it obstructs realization of innate divinity. This statement is not an endorsement of denial of wrongdoing or lack of regret for blunders. Rather, we must not overly identify with mistakes or convert justifiable remorse into excessive self-flagellation; that is a perversion of repentance. To repent means to own our errors fully and humbly and permanently turn away from them in thought, word, or deed, because they violate cosmic law and impede Self-realization.

Spirit rejoices when souls triumph over the beguiling allures of delusion. It is not easy to overcome the snares of ignorance and requires struggling against many seemingly natural impulses. Yet, as Saint Theresa of Avila counseled nuns of her order, "Do not be dismayed, daughters, at the number of things which you have to consider before setting out on this divine journey, which is the royal road to heaven. By taking this road we gain such precious treasures that it is no wonder if the cost seems to us a high one. The time will come when we shall realize that all we have paid has been nothing at all by comparison with the greatness of our prizes."[12] So, "Let nothing disturb thee: Let nothing dismay thee; All things pass; God never changes. Patience attains All that it strives for. He who has God finds he lacks nothing: God alone suffices."[13] Take heart, do your best, and trust in God. Spirit is not oblivious of our challenges. "Whenever virtue (dharma) declines and vice (adharma) predominates, I incarnate as an Avatar [descent of divinity into flesh]. In visible form

I appear from age to age to protect the virtuous and to destroy evildoing in order to reestablish righteousness."[14]

3

The Teacher: Finding an Enlightened Guide

The Buddhist tradition concisely and accurately identifies the basics for success on the spiritual path. These fundamentals are poetically called the Three Jewels and refer specifically to the Buddha, meaning an enlightened teacher; the Sangha, good and like-minded devotional companions; and the Dharma, eternal truth, cosmic law. Each plays a powerful role in spiritual development, and the principles they represent are relevant for all traditions in every age. We previously defined truth as the exact correspondence with absolute reality; in the next two chapters we will focus on the nature and function of the teacher and on good company, respectively.

THE ENLIGHTENED TEACHER

In the early stages of spiritual exploration, most people find value in basic instructors and books. Once their souls are sufficiently developed, God sends an enlightened teacher as a master or guru ("dispeller of darkness"). Masters are called such due to their having attained mastery over themselves, not others, and, if chosen to serve as a guru or illumined teacher, are divinely appointed to the task and not self-elected. They are chosen channels of sacred wisdom and holy power for all in spiritual need. Jesus is the guru of Christianity, as is Gautama in the Buddhist faith. Krishna, Rama, and others of similar attainment are revered in various Hindu sects. Enlightened masters are rare and despite being physically incarnate, they transcend ordinary mortal nature. Having achieved the highest degrees of Self-realization, they are liberated souls whose consciousness is united with God. No longer tainted by egoistic qualities that limit the pure expression of Spirit within them, they come solely to help others find illumination—salvation from the bondage of delusion.

Each master is appropriate for the select group of followers for whom they are sent. As Jesus stated, "No man can come to me, except the Father which hath sent me draw him: and I will raise him up at the last day."[1] This law of divine affinity attracts ripe souls to appropriate teachers when the time is right. Masters may serve small groups or world populations; the size of their following does not matter, nor does it change the quality of their attainment or the truth of their teaching. What matters is that they are legitimate. In the West we have seen various alleged Indian gurus usurp aspects of the classic master-disciple paradigm to swindle unwary followers of money, property, and sexual engagement. The same can be said of any cult leaders who control their flock for wrongful ends. These teachers are false, and nothing justifies their duplicity. The question arises, then, of how to select a genuine teacher. Since the consciousness of a master abides in spheres beyond ordinary human access, it sometimes takes one master to recognize another. Nevertheless, great teachers may be evaluated by three indicators: behavior, ability to manifest advanced states of consciousness at will, and the cultivation of saintly disciples—for, as the adage implies, trees are judged by their fruits.

We would not allow just anyone to take us mountain climbing; similarly, we should not follow another person gullibly just because he or she professes to be a spiritual adept or enlightened being. Talk is, as they say, cheap, and neophytes can be vulnerable to charismatic leaders or displays of miraculous powers, which, incidentally, have nothing to do with genuine spiritual stature. Prudent investigation is the best course to follow. Evaluate different paths, the founding masters, current leaders, and the body of teachings they expound. Much like choosing a life partner, test and evaluate before committing; develop familiarity with precepts and practices before entering into a deeper spiritual relationship. Proceed with alert deliberation, without rushing or feeling pressure to commit to any teacher or discipline that feels inappropriate. Gauge your feelings. Reflect to see if you are becoming a happier, better person by your own standards, and elicit objective feedback from persons you trust—not necessarily those within the group you are exploring. Practicing honest reflection and discrimination is extremely worthwhile and helps cultivate a crucial skill on the spiritual path: discernment. Masters and the tenets they impart must satisfy every aspect of a seeker's moral, rational, and spiritual scrutiny. You should not feel your integrity compromised or your intelligence minimized due to thoughtful inquiry or healthy skepticism. As we test gold to determine its value, so too must we evaluate masters, teachers, and teachings to determine their ability to help us reach God.

Though evaluating spiritual paths is prudent and necessary, it can, paradoxically, produce a kind of metaphysical indigestion, such as one might get by mixing rich foods. So when the right teaching and teacher are found, devote yourself to them enthusiastically. You will know what is right when the heart responds with a joyous intuitive recognition that dovetails with well-reasoned consideration. And, because quality of inner experience is more important than breadth of exposure, it is better to go deep with one teacher rather than to flit among many. Honor all paths, but be true to your own.

I found my master—or perhaps it was the other way around—after many years of unconscious seeking. As a youth, I felt drawn to charismatic persons who seemed wise but inevitably disillusioned me due to their inappropriate behaviors. After numerous disappointments, I opted never to follow anyone but a genuine master. Even after becoming enamored of

Autobiography of a Yogi, years passed before I recognized Yogananda as my guru. Reflecting on that moment, I recall receiving discipleship into his path and how it felt to do so:

I had been at the yoga retreat several weeks when a formal initiation ceremony was announced. Until then, I had been casually enjoying the novelty of my experience, but that was about to change. The opportunity I was being given to receive discipleship to a master was not a matter to take lightly. My notification of the event came at the last minute. With scant time for reflection, I quickly reviewed what I had experienced over time and intuitively recognized a profound sense of rightness, a feeling of spiritual belonging with Yogananda and his teachings. His was an authentic practice and worldview that I could fully embrace.

The ceremony itself was not complex. Participants were simply asked whether they wished to become disciples on this path. For the record, such rituals are not common in the Yogananda tradition, but this one helped clarify my intent, so I joined in. When it came time for me to respond, I felt a distinct hush come upon me. The universe seemed to be holding its breath, mutely asserting, "You alone must make this decision; no influence shall sway your free will." I chose discipleship and subsequently felt enveloped by a rare and sacred bond. To this day I consider finding a true teacher the most valuable thing one can do.

Master teachers are not chosen by personal whim. They are God-appointed conduits of divine wisdom and grace uniquely suited for each soul. The relationship between master and disciple exists exclusively, and over many lifetimes if need be, to transform receptive devotees into liberated souls. I have been asked many times about whether having a master is necessary to attain salvation. While some feel the answer is no, every culture has some form of spiritual apprenticeship when mystical knowledge is sought. Yogananda stated that, as a divine law, the spiritual liberation of the soul required the facilitation of a guru. John the Baptist performed this function for Jesus (more on that later), thereby fulfilling a sacred mandate or "all righteousness."[2]

In the West, people accept special training in graduate school or professional sports without a second thought. They understand that the higher one climbs in any field, the greater the teacher must be to nurture their skills. In spiritual matters, oddly, there is a curious disconnect in accepting this dynamic. The ego protects its cherished whims and infatuations, likes and dislikes, cloaking them in the guise of personal relevance. To surrender one's egoistic bias and humbly confront the innumerable conditionings that obscure and confound one's soul requires great strength of character. Just as we submit to qualified doctors for surgical procedures, we must likewise purify the self. This process requires the incisive ability of one flawlessly attuned to Spirit, a master, to help transmute lesions of ego into soul realization. Associating with a master also provides the opportunity to raise one's consciousness to levels of insight not ordinarily possible. Such association is the metaphysical relevance of the parable of the bridegroom: "Then came to him the disciples of John, saying, 'Why do we and the Pharisees fast oft, but thy disciples fast not?' And Jesus said unto them, 'Can the children of the bridechamber mourn, as long as the bridegroom is with them?' but the days will come, when the bridegroom shall be taken from them, and then shall they fast."[3]

Spiritual practice lifts one Godward. A master's vibrational field is such that close disciples may temporarily drop intense spiritual efforts because the Divine is readily accessible to them by being in the presence of their master. Once a master dies, however, consciousness-elevating disciplines must be resumed. What is imperative is for disciples to practice receptivity to the emanations that flow through masters regardless of whether the latter are physically present or not. This necessity was conveyed in the statement, "But as many as received him, to them gave he power to become the sons of God."[4] The real trick is learning to remain receptively attuned to God while engaging in spiritual practices like meditation and also performing daily duties.

This next story recounts another man's search for a genuine spiritual master. A keenly intelligent, highly motivated man once traveled throughout his native India asking various teachers if they knew God. After repeated disappointments, one saintly man finally answered yes. This exalted soul was Sri Ramakrishna. The dubious seeker decided to test the saint and did so—at every opportunity for many years—lest he be duped in some fashion. Of these tests Ramakrishna said, "You must test me as the money-changers test their coins. You mustn't accept me until you've tested me thoroughly."[5] Despite intense and perpetual scrutiny, the man failed to detect any shortcomings. Finally he spied Ramakrishna sneaking off at night, naked, into the woods. Thinking to catch him in an amorous liaison, the man followed behind. What his spying revealed was something considerably different: Ramakrishna fled into the forest nude, true, but solely to meditate in babe-like surrender to the Divine Mother. Finally satisfied, the man accepted Ramakrishna as his guru. The person in this story became Swami Vivekananda, Ramakrishna's foremost disciple. When reflecting on this process, Vivekananda said, "I fought my Master for six long years, with the result that I know every inch of the way."[6]

Because the spiritual arena, like psychotherapy, is fraught with the blessings and perils of intense vulnerability, I want to reiterate certain previously addressed matters of critical importance. Foremost, trust yourself and judge wisely. Be prudent in your assessment of a teacher, and do not hesitate to heed your own counsel.

It is not unusual to test various paths while searching for your own, and, unfortunately, not all teachers are honorable. Seekers can engage with leaders in extremely intimate contexts that, if mishandled, can have devastating consequences. False teachers can deceive in subtle ways that distort philosophies of devotion, loyalty, and obedience into exploitive platforms of power and submission. The unwary may be susceptible to financial exploitation, sexual abuse, or, worse, brainwashing that ruptures familial or familiar ties and sometimes compromises rationality. Given the series of sex-related scandals involving religious figures in recent years, one book worth reviewing is *Sex and the Spiritual Teacher* by Scott Edelstein (Wisdom Press, 2011). It covers useful information that can help the ignorant or naïve avoid damaging incidents. Another resource is *Where to Draw the Line: How to Set Healthy Boundaries Every Day* by Anne Katherine (Fireside, 2000). Forewarned *is* forearmed, so when in doubt about any teacher or group, remember these four maxims:

Do not allow yourself to stop thinking rationally or feeling freely.

Do not cut off ties with family, friends, or things that interest you.

Do not give away large sums of money or material possessions.

Do not have sex with your spiritual teacher or guide.

If you are trying to convince yourself to follow a path despite internal misgivings, your intuition is undoubtedly warning you—stay clear! Honor cautionary signals; do not become beguiled by ensnaring ploys. Move on. Yogananda's master, Swami Sri Yukteswar, provided sterling counsel for aspiring spiritual disciples when he said, "Many teachers will tell you to believe; then they put out your eyes of reason and instruct you to follow only their logic. But I want you to keep your eyes of reason open; in addition, I will open in you another eye, the eye of wisdom."[7] Memorize that statement; it is the benchmark of what a true master expects and depicts the quality of character by which to assess other teachers. Yukteswar also stated, "If you don't like my words, you are at liberty to leave at any time. . . . I want nothing from you but your own improvement. Stay only if you feel benefited."[8] Such is the counsel of a sage.

I can personally attest that one need not speak to a guru to receive his or her teachings; just being in an enlightened teacher's presence is a profoundly transforming and uplifting experience. The powerful, high-consciousness energy field that an authentic guru transmits is tangible, especially if one has been practicing yoga (a spiritual discipline) for some time.

As rightly noted above, genuine masters of any spiritual tradition need not be incarnate to offer spiritual protection and guidance. Embodiment may give a personal flavor to boost a disciple's training, but masters aren't "dead" or ineffective simply because they have left the earth. Their reality is of conscious unity with Spirit unhindered by physical form. Merged in the eternal, they are beyond limitation. Masters can create bodily forms in vision or flesh whenever they wish. If they do, these manifestations serve as familiar ways to make contact and are reserved for unique, divinely sanctioned situations. Jesus did this for Saint Francis, as did Sri Yukteswar for Yogananda.

When a living master cannot be found, do not despair. Select a path established by a previously incarnate master that best resonates with you, and follow it. You may also find a seasoned instructor who provides beneficial spiritual direction despite not being fully illumined. This approach is appropriate if the teacher renders quality aid without false claims about his or her own status. Wisdom from any source is still wisdom; many teachers are advanced in their field and able to offer valuable insight and service. The important thing in such cases is to heed your mentor while trying to deepen an inner link with the Divine. If and when it is right for you to develop a spiritual relationship with a genuine master, you will know it. While attempting to do so, however, do not be fooled by so-called psychics who claim to channel exalted beings. They are deluded. True masters leave legacies on earth for all to see; postscripts are not necessary. Yogananda explained that the spiritual vibrational field of a realized being is so intense that it cannot be channeled except by another soul of similar spiritual elevation. Less developed nervous systems would be overtaxed. It would be like directing current from a power plant into a house without transformers to step down the voltage—all the circuits would fry. Furthermore, masters do not reply to spurious psychic summons but to prayer, meditation, and attunement with the path they founded. Once we recognize that the realm of Spirit is ever present and omnipresent, the loving remembrance of God or his saints becomes doorways to their presence. The capacity to tune in to an illumined one or Spirit is just a devotional thought away.

THE INNER TEACHER

As mentioned earlier, some individuals bristle at the notion of following anyone on the spiritual path, considering disciplines that challenge cherished habits or beliefs an anathema. In such cases, their resistance may take the form of a dubious obeisance to the inner teacher. The inner teacher is a potentially viable resource but must be considered cautiously, as it may just be a sophisticated form of self-deception. Its proponents are usually too blinded by sentimental fallacies to tease fact from fancy; they perpetuate error-prone dalliances with subconscious projections under the guise of following the inner teacher rather than doing what is required to cultivate reliable soul guidance. Though ego purification can be daunting at times, it is fundamentally why "outer" teachers, masters, are so valuable: They give what is needed, when it is relevant—accurate guidance and discipline to achieve realization. If we find such prodding too difficult or unattractive at times, that does not diminish its merit.

For those sufficiently advanced, the inner teacher is an honorable reality. It is God, the ultimate guru, speaking through the still, quiet voice within—soul intuition. As frequently stated, intuition is the soul's capacity to discern the truth directly without intermediary input of the physical senses. We all possess an intuitive ability and should develop it, yet it becomes flawless only after one has fully transmuted the ego, and doing so takes disciplined training. An outer teacher is no longer necessary once perfect attunement to divine wisdom is achieved. From that point onward, spiritual adepts can successfully access the inner teacher, God, because they are sufficiently refined to receive its subtle guidance accurately. This caveat does not mean people should avoid seeking inner direction until fully illumined. Were that the case, we would all likely remain waiting endlessly or rely exclusively on dubious authority figures—something hierarchal religious systems would greatly appreciate! Rather, we should cultivate intuition while acknowledging that the fine nuances of Spirit are seldom grasped by those of flawed insight or ego-blinded natures. Whoever seeks wisdom must also recognize when external guidance is necessary. Such an attitude displays humility, a quality needed to cultivate insight and protect against deceptive self-sufficiency. Fortunately, no genuine teacher micromanages disciples, and there are opportunities aplenty to learn from our choices and our mistakes. When a master provides counsel, though, it is wise for students to pay heed. When a seeker no longer requires a master's guidance—and such situations do occur—she or he will be duly informed.

4

Good Company: Spiritual Community

The essential value of spiritual community is twofold: support for those seeking inner advancement and protection against oppositional delusive forces. The community principle also has two aspects, one subtle and the other tangible. The first aspect is of an energetic nature, whereby a potent vibrational field is generated through holy practices that neutralize negative influences. Anything related to God—devotion, service, prayer, or meditation—emits a high-frequency electromagnetic field that elevates—or spiritualizes—whoever falls within its range of influence. Accordingly, group participation in sacred activities is synergistically uplifting for everyone involved. Recognizing these realities and their value to spiritual aspirants, my master stressed that environment is a stronger force than willpower. He also warned that the laws of vibratory exchange are degrading if the company kept is not good. Therefore, a key benefit of good community is subtle reinforcement of divine pursuits and corresponding inoculation against corrupting forces. Worldly temptation promises much but delivers little. Its glamour is like fool's gold—shiny, yet lacking true value. Spirit alone is perpetually all satisfying and good.

On a tangible level, participation in spiritual community affords access to goods, services, and resources—social or otherwise—that make it easier to live a God-centered life. When I once asked a monk why he lived in a cloistered society, he said it was easier for him to remain focused on God. For him, the sequestered life provided more gratifying friendships, activities, and focus than an ordinary worldly life. However, all sincere enthusiasts do not need to flock to hermitages; that would be impractical. Rather, the deliberate choice to engage spiritually minded associates for companionship or professional services lets one fashion a kind of insulation against worldly temperaments. For instance, I am keenly aware of the energetic "residue" left by tradespersons who have worked in my house. As such, I make a deliberate effort to hire or refer those who are conscientious and high-minded. And in this age of electronic media, there is nothing amiss with applying spiritual principles to online social-networking.

Good company is not defined by group size as much as by quality of character. It can exist in small gatherings or large organizations. Intimate spiritual assemblies often have an informal flavor that appeals to some, while larger institutional groups provide different benefits. Interestingly, Yogananda initially resisted building a spiritual organization until his guru said, "God is the Honey, organizations are the hives; both are necessary. Any form is useless, of course, without the spirit, but why not start busy hives full of the spiritual nectar?"[1] The challenge with any organization dedicated to the Divine is keeping the spirit alive, maintaining quality, yet not succumbing to operational mandates that stifle growth rather than promote it. Spiritual community, then, is fundamentally only as good as its energy, which stems from right attitude and input, not size or affectation. One dedicated soul is better than a crowd of curiosity seekers, but a crowd of dedicated souls is better still.

While spiritual associations are undeniably valuable, anything involving personalities can have downsides. As such, well-meaning groups are still susceptible to the influence of toxic behaviors, the most pernicious of which are the inclination to judge, isolationism, and misdirection. Harsh judgment is common from those with a dogmatic tendency who are threatened by whoever deviates from the status quo. Rigid adherence to perceived paradigms has little, if anything, to do with group doctrine and more to do with insecurity. Judgmental types promote ideas that buttress apprehensions and try to squelch independent-minded thinkers who do not conform to their sense of propriety. A positive by-product of these individuals is the chance to practice tolerant fearlessness: "Judgmentalists" must be confronted lest their behavior erode group harmony or reduce membership. Still, there are no reasons to shun organizations outright. Simply be mindful that humans are, by nature, works in process. Avoiding a group is advisable only if truth and free will are suppressed within the group. If organizations transgress cosmic law and the sanctity of being human, they should be renounced.

The second toxic behavior, isolationism, refers to a dated ideal of needing to leave society in order to be spiritual. There may have been periods in history when retreat from society was necessary to foster inner growth, but not now. In this age, we practice sacred principles within frameworks of complex lives and understand that spiritual development results from soul realization and not physical setting. Attachment to isolated community may suggest an inability to engage with others or an escapist tendency to flee from life traumas. If such is the case, reclusiveness is not spiritually helpful; it reflects psychosocial denial. Clearly, locale does not axiomatically foster sanctity; folly exists in cloistered environs as well as in urban ones. It is how we think, feel, and act regardless of our setting that counts. Cultivation of a proper inner environment—right thought and corresponding behavior—is what matters most. Here is an anecdote based on an autobiographical story by Japanese Zen master Tanzan (1819–1892) that makes this point delightfully:

One day, the abbot of a Zen monastery and his monastic companion were returning from a pilgrimage when they saw a woman stranded at a stream bank. Rains had flooded the area so she could not cross the water without ruining her clothes. The abbot offered to carry her to the opposite side; the other monk remained aloof. The woman accepted the assistance and after being put down gratefully went her way. Several hours passed until the monk could not contain himself any longer. Exasperated, he asked the abbot, "What were you doing? We have taken strict vows of celibacy, yet there you were in intimate physical contact with a woman!"

The abbot smiled and replied, "I merely offered assistance to one in need, and, although I indeed carried a woman's body for ten yards and in chaste spirit, you have carried her, and me, with judgmental thoughts these past twelve miles!"

The choice for a sequestered lifestyle must arise from a natural calling and inclination, not from fear, obligation, or a sense of necessity. Spiritual work requires applying what we have learned in all aspects of daily life regardless of where we are, not using faulty notions of residential elitism as benchmarks of merit.

Finally, there is the issue of misdirection. Groups may be formed around profound teachings yet lack counselors who provide quality guidance. In such instances, poor advice can be ineffective or injurious. For example, Saint Theresa of Avila once received priestly counsel that dismissed her mystical experiences as satanic. Because she was loyal to her cloister's spiritual-guidance process, she temporarily shunned unfolding divine revelations and later regretted it. Fortunately, a subsequent spiritual director refuted the earlier finding and pronounced her experiences to be profoundly holy. Saint Theresa suffered for heeding the first counselor's ignorant advice because she was more advanced than he. With aid from the second advocate, she realized that it was better to follow her own sacred insights.

In short, spiritual guidance must be provided only by those able to give it. When done well, it clarifies, ennobles, and uplifts. It helps the soul understand its path more clearly and is accompanied by a sense of rightness or joyful, intuitive resonance that reflects alignment with truth. Even when errors are discussed, they are addressed kindly and used to promote beneficial understanding. When counsel is mishandled, it causes pain, fear, or confusion—constrictive fruits of the blind leading the uncertain. This situation should be avoided. The wise recognize what is needed and how to deliver it, whereas poor guidance can mislead, hurt, or support error. In spiritual communities, there are always those willing to lend an ear or offer an opinion, so be wary of whom you seek counsel from, and be mindful to heed only the feedback that rings true.

An experience directly related to this happened to me at the conclusion of my yoga teacher training. Uncertain about what to do next or where to go, I fell into an immobilizing period of indecision. I sought innumerable opinions, which, naturally, invited innumerable responses. Some were vitalizing; others were not. Poor self-confidence and susceptibility to peer input exacerbated my inability to trust my instincts. This internal environment perpetuates stasis and in foul circumstances can be harnessed by malicious people or groups to ensnare the susceptible. Fortunately, I was not fated with anything worse than seeing the futility of not making choices. Maturity requires taking responsibility, and it is better to err honoring one's truth than to subscribe to another's views or to wallow endlessly in uncertainty. If that means making blunders, so be it. The world will not end if we err, and sometimes we must make wrong decisions to recognize right ones and then correct ourselves accordingly. Making mistakes is part of life, but refusing to learn from them is a greater problem. As long as we grow from missteps, they may be our greatest teachers, not our greatest failures. Wisdom is born of experience, and there is nothing like the dance of life to teach us what we need to know.

An important issue related to spiritual guidance merits mentioning here. There is a purifying process associated with inner growth that may trigger mental, emotional, or psychic experiences and require professional counseling to address. There is no shame in this. We are multifaceted beings who harbor conflicted feelings and buried memories. Consequently, when inner pursuits draw upon increased levels of energy and attention, subconscious impurities may rise to the surface of conscious awareness for healing. Much like clarifying butter, the fire of spiritual practice can cause impurities to bubble up for removal. That is a gift. The process may take time but inevitably results in a purified product and, in this case, delivers a more refined, fully integrated you. I once had a period during which I experienced panic attacks. I contacted a spiritual counselor to discuss these matters, but he had no idea what to do or how to help me. For those familiar with internal upheaval, panic episodes are not rare or uncommon. My contact was out of his depth. Familiarity with sacred teachings does not automatically make one a good counselor, and ignorance, be it temporal or spiritual, serves no one. To advise rightly, one must have insight into the full spectrum of human nature and effectively apply spiritual teachings to diverse life circumstances. Spirituality is not a ticket out of pain but a choice to embrace what comes in life consciously and with integrity.

In concluding this chapter, it must be noted that the value of harmonious spiritual associations is undeniable. The vibrational power of shared magnetism is an invaluable developmental aid serving to protect the saplings of inner aspirations against the marauding animals of tempting delusion. Still, life is unique for everyone. If being more solitary and not participating in group functions feels right, do not discount that. Spiritual disciplines are meant to promulgate beneficial principles and should not corrode enthusiastic practice by inflexible rigidity; they ought to guide practitioners in alignment with their nature and needs. Whatever choices confront you—selecting a teacher, a path, or a group— do what expedites Self-realization. You cannot go too far astray if you intelligently, mindfully, and intuitionally keep your eye on the singular goal, God.

5

The Twelve Principles of Spiritual Understanding

Enlightenment does not come without ongoing devotional effort and commitment. The pull of worldly attraction is extreme; it fuels our natural tendency to look outwardly for a fulfillment that is essentially within us. The continual tug-of-war between the instinctual aspects of human bodies and the subtle elements of being a soul forms the battleground upon which the struggle for spiritual illumination must be fought. In such a context, the Three Jewels referenced previously, the teacher, the truth, and community, provide ideal elements to support inner awakening. Truth seekers receive wisdom from qualified teachers, engage in soul-revealing practices, and enjoy the benefits associated with uplifting fellowship.

In addition to the Three Jewels, there are twelve principles that enrich spiritual growth and understanding. They are universal realities rooted in cosmic law.

1. We are not mortal beings seeking to be spiritual, but eternal souls reclaiming what we already are.

2. Anything causing or promoting a sense of separation from God is delusory.

3. Creation is the externalized manifestation, or body, of God.

4. The universe, being of Spirit, hence connected to all creation, is effectively our larger Self.

5. God has a dual nature that operates by law and grace. We must obey the law and attract the grace.

6. The proper attitude for spiritual practice is unconditional love and surrender to God.

7. Free will can be tuned to divine will for enlightenment or misused to remain in delusion.

8. No one can gain Self-realization for us. Spiritual effort is our responsibility.

9. Powers and miracles do not reflect knowledge of God, nor do they impart salvation.

10. God alone must be the object of worship.

11. Eight classic qualities of God are light, sound, wisdom, power, love, peace, calmness, and joy.

12. Spiritual progress, though subtle, is measurable in definite ways.

Let us look at these principles one by one.

1. *We are not mortal beings seeking to be spiritual, but eternal souls reclaiming what we already are.*

When we are in unfamiliar territory, maps help us to chart courses toward destinations. Of course, for any map to be effective it must have a starting and ending point. This analogy also applies to life. People who believe they exist without rhyme or reason are effectively lost in unfamiliar territory. They live without context, confused, and bereft of higher purpose. Isolation from correct spiritual ideology often fosters ignorant, self-defeating behaviors that are largely responsible for many personal or societal ills. To correct this situation and navigate away from its unsavory terrain, a paradigm must be embraced that acknowledges we are not biological accidents but souls derived of Spirit. Something cannot come from nothing, and, as sparks fly from fire, every spark of life or soul is a microcosmic, individual aspect of the universal flame of life from which it originated. As sparks are essentially identical to their source, so too are we essentially identical to our Creator. The belief that we are but physical beings, finite, mortal, and perishable, is false. We are of Spirit and as such *are* Spirit. Once created, we never cease to be, nor can our sacred constitution be destroyed. The god in us can never be diminished or obliterated. We are eternal units of the Divine and shall be so evermore. This is the spiritual truth that transforms existential meaninglessness into intentional existence and reveals life to be definitive and holy. Awareness clarified through divine remembrance shows that we never pursued Spirit to gain anything other than the realization of what we already are—divine. "Is it not written in your law, I said, Ye are gods?"[1]

2. *Anything causing or promoting a sense of separation from God is delusory.*

A recurring theme in the twelve principles is that everything is part of Spirit and nothing is apart from it. All contrary perceptions are delusory. Delusion, though, is a necessary aspect of creation; it is the way by which distinction—a sense of multiplicity—is formed. The universal tapestry could not be woven unless an appearance of separateness existed. While the infinite is fundamentally composed of one thing, Spirit, illusory veils of differentiation form the requisite backdrop upon which creation can be made manifest. Spirit projects delusive distinctions to sustain creation while simultaneously seeking to draw everything back to itself. In Vedic terms, this cosmic propulsion out, then reversion back, is called *lila*, the unfathomable divine play. We are situationally compelled to cognize diversity, then, eventually, to see past it to perceive underlying divine unity. Delusion directs consciousness away from apprehending oneness, so its influence is readily detected by a sense of separation from Spirit. Accordingly, all spiritual traditions encourage participants to reject ill-wrought feelings of disconnection from the Creator and affirm being ever part of That-Which-Abides. "I am the Lord, and there is none else, there is no God beside me. . . . I form the light, and create darkness: I make peace, and create evil: I the Lord do all these things."[2]

3. Creation is the externalized manifestation, or body, of God.

One definition for the universe is "the totality of known or supposed objects and phenomena throughout space."[3] This interpretation is fine but lacks any reference to what caused the universe. For that I cite two comparable scriptural passages:

> For by him were all things created, that are in heaven, and that are in earth, visible and invisible, whether they be thrones, or dominions, or principalities, or powers: all things were created by him, and for him.[4]

> I am the Progenitor and also the Dissolver of the entire cosmos.
> O Arjuna! There is nothing higher than Me, or beyond Me. All
> things (creatures and objects) are bound to Me like a row of gems
> on a thread.[5]

The Bible states that creation is the Almighty's handiwork. The Bhagavad Gita refines this point further by specifying that the universe is fashioned of thought projected from Spirit's consciousness. The biblical view can be accepted without believing an Eastern model, but both are compatible. Physics asserts that matter and energy are interchangeable. Metaphysicians and (some) quantum physicists rank thought as a subtler component of this same continuum. The term *body* can be dryly defined as a physical structure or the material substance of an animal, plant, person, object in space, or main mass of anything living or created. Such being the case, we need look no further than nature's entirety to perceive the invisible Creator made visible. Spirit is not hidden, but ever present and all-pervasive, the cosmic source and its substance. All creation manifests the Body Divine, complete with the infinite intelligence that permeates and directs it. There is also said to be an unmanifest aspect of Spirit, which exists without form and beyond the realm of creation. This transcendent component is not separate from the Creator but is known solely through highest spiritual realization.

4. Being of Spirit, hence connected to all creation, the universe is also our larger Self.

When you watch a movie, visual effects result from fluctuations of light projected on a screen. Similarly, when uniquely shaped molds are filled with water and frozen, they still hold one thing: ice. This is the crux of creation: Spirit projects itself in various ways onto a screen of duality. Despite diverse roles and appearances, humanity and nature are intimately related because we are made of the same stuff, Spirit. Since nature is the body of God, it correspondingly comprises our macrocosmic Self.

Native Americans, among many others, have said as much for ages. To quote Chief Seattle, "All things share the same breath—the beast, the tree, the man—the air shares its spirit with all the life it supports."[6] Illusions of separateness from all matter and life dissolve in states of expanded awareness referred to as cosmic consciousness or samadhi. We experience oneness with the universe and literally perceive it as our colossal Self. We truly are connected.

Many people have an intuitive sense of this reality. In my case, I recall hiking in Norway when suddenly I was able to sense trees, spaces between them, and the location of boulders—all with closed eyes. This sensitivity grew over time until I could feel the presence of life emerging in trees and plants during springtime. Such impressions are neither unique nor imaginary but perceptions of a fundamental force that integrates our individual form with every form. Such empathic observations validate the ability to identify with the One Life; all one need do is pay attention, as did the famed naturalist John Muir: "When we try to pick out anything by itself, we find it hitched to everything else in the Universe."[7]

5. God has a dual nature that operates by law and grace. We must obey the law and attract the grace.

Principles of duality pervade creation, and Spirit operates accordingly through cosmic law and grace. In Taoism, these principles are loosely referred to as yin and yang. Interestingly, certain aspects of these qualities are evident in stereotypical gender attributes because, as microcosms of Spirit, people manifest divine attributes in miniature. Male, or yang, attributes generally express rational, analytical, exacting behaviors that epitomize cosmic law. For example, fathers commonly expect strict adherence to domestic rules or impose punishing consequences if they are not obeyed. They "lay down the law." Such is the nature of cosmic order: obey or pay. This divine aspect governs impersonally and with mathematical precision; emotion does not enter the equation.

Seeking divine union via cosmic law requires mental detachment and attentiveness to behavioral subtleties so exacting that perfect compliance with them becomes nigh on impossible. Even the Bhagavad Gita concedes, "Those whose goal is the Unmanifested [the transcendent, unemotionally operative law aspect] increase the difficulties; arduous is the path to the Absolute for embodied beings."[8]

Although Spirit may be approached as law, it can never be compelled to bestow liberation. That comes by grace alone, the form of responsiveness attributed to the personal, feminine, or yin, quality of Spirit. Just as female archetypes are generally depicted as feeling, compassionate, and nurturing, so does the Divine Mother shelter and love her children regardless of their errant ways. Kuan Yin, the bodhisattva of compassion, whose name roughly translates as "the one who hears the cries of the world," epitomizes this divine feminine attribute. So, fundamentally, redemptive grace may be petitioned from the personal aspect of Spirit and not its impersonal one.

This rule of thumb need not be considered absolute. Judeo-Christian faiths favor God as Father while Hindus enjoy Divine as Mother, yet both seek the love, compassion, mercy, forgiveness, and grace arising from an intimately personal exchange with Spirit. In short, though all genuine worship is good, those who venerate Spirit as the formless Absolute may find it hard to love an impersonal concept that is far beyond human cognition. And without love, spiritual progress is arrested because love attracts that upon which it focuses. Adoration of a personified Godhead provides the mind and heart with imagery that fosters reverence. Love is the secret power of devotion; its magnetic pull draws the redeeming grace of Spirit. "A man attains perfection by worshipping, with his natural gifts, Him from whom all beings are evolved, and by whom all this world is permeated."[9] Human nature craves relationship, and even nontheistic traditions like Buddhism incorporate various masters or personal deities, like Kuan Yin, for help in attaining liberation. Again, the personified Spirit motif appears to be the ideal model for realizing the Sacred regardless of faith system.

It is important to emphasize that adherence to cosmic law is necessary despite the overarching value of grace. Cosmic laws govern universal operations on macrocosmic and microcosmic levels and must be obeyed to optimize collective function and individual growth. Unfortunately, ignorance of these laws—and some are exceedingly subtle—brings undesirable consequences. Given the intricacy of this system, it can be daunting for humans always to know how to behave. So we are gifted with a feedback system to keep us on track: karma, the law of cause and effect. Though an Eastern term, karma is a universal precept referred to in Western scripture in passages such as, "Be not deceived; God is not mocked: for whatsoever a man soweth, that shall he also reap."[10]

Understanding karma more thoroughly can help us navigate life more dexterously because it is a process that governs individuals, societies, and civilizations. It is not a frivolous or hurtful rule like the counterfeit "You create your own reality" paradigm that distorts karmic principles with inaccurate magical thinking. Rather, karmic law is a precise response mechanism that guides spiritual evolution. Harmony reigns when we heed cosmic law; suffering ensues when we do not. Karma is not limited to one lifetime but spans multiple lives, a premise some may not easily accept. Yet it is the only viable explanation behind the vast disparities in existence. Universal operations are mathematically precise, exacting, and impartial, yet ever fair. It is human shortsightedness that fails to perceive causative factors behind the mysterious circumstances we experience and, usually, decry. Knowing we are measured by a system of infallible divine assessment can help us cease externalizing blame for unwelcome events and prompt the mending of self-created fates by altering trends of thought and deeds that initiate or perpetuate outcomes. No one can be blamed for our circumstances; we alone are accountable. This is an empowering point if understood correctly because when responsibility is wisely applied, it leads to freedom.

Application of this precept requires thinking before acting and being mindful of outcomes. Just as health laws contribute to fitness, spiritual laws result in Self-realization. Karma inevitably prompts us to live in ways that lift the veil of delusion from the soul. It is important not to get disheartened when unpleasant situations arise. All of us have weeds in our inner gardens as well as flowers. Unpredictable events happen in life, as do our unpolished responses to them. Personal transformation requires commitment to vigilant equilibrium and remaining centered in soul consciousness despite life's karmic ups and downs. Change what you can as you can. The famed Serenity Prayer puts it well: "God grant me the serenity to accept the things I cannot change, courage to change the things I can, and wisdom to know the difference." On a lighter note, life is mysterious, so don't take it so seriously. We cannot always impact our circumstances, but we can choose how to respond to them.

The principle of attracting grace is extremely significant, for it is deemed necessary to attain salvation. Various traditions view grace differently, yet it is generally considered the merited or unmerited mercy of God. I describe grace as an ever-flowing, merciful force of Spirit, whose outpouring is increased by the magnetic pull of devotion. It has been said that God cannot resist the heart's divinely directed love and responds to sincere soul calls. To attract redemptive grace, then, two things are needed: love for God and a shift in our perspective from estrangement to intimacy. Attitudes that keep God at bay must be rejected. As parents give generously to their offspring yet do little for strangers, so we must affirm our status as children of Spirit and demand salvation. This practice reflects an attitude of justifiable entitlement, an inherent birthright that is not afforded those who deem themselves unworthy outsiders. To claim God's redeeming aid, we must do so as rightly deserving divine children, a disposition that reflects the soul's true birthright and just due.

The word *demand* usually implies command or arrogance but here conveys loving intimacy. Children unrepentantly make demands of their parents. They do not mean to be arrogant; they simply expect their mothers or fathers to be there for them. And they are. So is God. In many faith systems, however, people are taught to pray as beggars, a practice that hinders spiritual growth because it reinforces the lie of separation. Children, again, have no problem asserting themselves when they feel securely loved. Engagement with God should be no different. Therefore, we need to reconfigure our relationship with the Divine into one of loving, rightful intimacy in order to demand salvation. Spiritual forces are bound to assist the soul's progress home when we do so and heed cosmic law to the best of our abilities.

6. *The proper attitude for spiritual practice is unconditional love and surrender to God.*

Building on the concept of grace, it is said that Spirit has everything but the freely offered love of our souls. This love is the only thing it craves and the one item we can bestow. Though never forced to give affection, spiritual effort becomes most effective when the Divine has top priority in our lives. The reason for this is metaphysical. Mind can direct consciousness like sunlight through a magnifying glass and incinerate the apparent separateness between things by focused concentration. When this happens, the mind merges with the object of its attention. Applying this practice to spiritual matters, complete concentration on

Spirit is necessary to unite with it. Mechanically speaking, love draws energy to the heart, where it can be routed to centers of divine realization in the brain. If love exists conditionally, the heart will not open fully and the capacity to channel its force is compromised. Only by unconditional love and total surrender can the cumulative elements of consciousness and energy be perfectly directed to Spirit. Without that, divine union is unattainable. It must also be remembered that we are Spirit; any mindset that subverts this realization impedes Self-knowing. Therefore, sacred practices should be done with attentive love, not dryness or distraction. As Krishna told his disciple Arjuna, "On Me fix thy mind, be thou My devotee, with ceaseless worship bow reverently before Me. Having thus united thyself to Me as thy Highest Goal, thou shalt be Mine own."[11]

Despite our holy essence, most people balk at loving God. They wonder how reverential attitudes can be cultivated for a seemingly intangible Spirit. The answer can be initially resolved through imagination. Affection flows readily to whatever we enjoy: friends, lovers, natural beauty. Yet all are manifestations of the Divine. Perceiving God as the source and form of whatever we care for lets us apply personal feelings toward the otherwise mysterious Creator. Envisioning Spirit in this manner provides a sense of closeness to it from which enduring relationships can be cultivated. Seekers can eventually know Spirit directly through increasingly deep realizations born of meditation. Until then, it is useful to practice the presence of God and believe what innumerable saints have professed, that God is nearer than the near and dearer than the dear. Whoever thinks him distant, he will be so; yet whoever thinks him near, he is. The thought of God is the gateway to his presence; unconditional loving surrender is the soul's road home.

7. Free will can be attuned to divine will for enlightenment or misused to remain in delusion.

Free will is a blessing and a challenge. We can harness it to soar to the heights of realization or use it to sink into depravity. Since our fundamental earthly purpose is to awaken spiritually, right use of will consists in doing just that. Wrong use of will consists in acting against our highest good and perpetuates delusion. Years may be spent engaged in ill-advised deeds until a sour harvest is reaped, so the challenge of free will is learning how to use it properly. But what exactly is will? As with any tool, there is a reason it was fashioned and a correct purpose to which it should be applied. It is the instrument that operates the body/mind: the force of conscious intention that directs energy into action. In babies, will is chiefly organic and responsive to basic urges. Toddlers with more self-awareness usually assert will rashly, just because they can. Teens or young adults tend to engage willpower brashly or to fulfill desires, some of questionable merit. Eventually, a point is reached where wisdom, not whim, guides will. Wisdom is action or knowledge attuned to divine law. When human will is perfectly aligned with wisdom, it is identical to divine will. Jesus demonstrated perfected will in his trial at the Garden of Gethsemane when he overcame personal preferences and surrendered to divine will: "O my Father, if this cup may not pass away from me, except I drink it, thy will be done."[12] The result was his crucifixion. Although an exceptional case, it demonstrates a critical point: God gave us will to use, not forsake. Surrender of will does not mean abandoning free choice but aligning it to divine purpose. The highest use of will, then, is ultimately for personal liberation and the salvation of others.

Saints and masters demonstrate attunement with divine will because they make the effort to do so. Most of us do not. As a result, we frequently pilot ourselves into troubled waters. To counter this tendency, we must learn to access higher guidance through intuition and then apply it appropriately. The former is achieved with meditation and prayer, when consciousness becomes clarified and soul insight becomes discernable. The latter is accomplished by the disciplined, dispassionate exercise of intention to execute intuitive directives. As in Jesus's struggle, this is not always easy to do. However, the more we harness these faculties, the more wisely we live and eventually become masters of ourselves.

The following exercise enhances intuition and helps us develop right use of will. Use it for significant decisions or general life issues or, more importantly, for steering a correct course toward illumination.

Close your eyes, calm yourself, and silently affirm, "I and my Heavenly Father are one!" Use a term for the Divine that best suits you—Heavenly Father, Spirit, Divine Mother, or another. Repeat this affirmation continuously with full attention until you feel a great joy in the heart. Then lovingly and repeatedly demand guidance for issues, needs, or questions you have until that heart joy feels overflowing. Now stop the demand process. Become still. Sensitively feel for intuitive images, subtle insights, or other inner responses. Do not anticipate outcomes; maintain emotional neutrality and be receptive. Do not despair if nothing presents itself. Remain confident and faithful. Spirit often answers mysteriously and in unforeseen ways. You may find people saying things uncannily relevant to your concern or stumble upon written material of similar merit. These are divine replies. Whatever comes, know that authentic divine guidance is verified by a sense of rightness or joy in the heart. Any sense of fear, doubt, heaviness, or negativity indicates what to avoid. Again, discernment of these matters takes time to cultivate yet eventually can be relied upon to align life choices with divine will. Perfecting the process is a learning adventure, but be assured that right intentions will inevitably engender right results if correctly exercised.

8. No one can attain Self-realization for us. Spiritual effort is our responsibility.

Self-effort in the Christian tradition is often misunderstood due in large part to misinterpretation of the New Testament passage, "But as many as received him, to them gave he power to become the sons of God, even to them that believe on his name."[13] According to that statement, spiritual merit can be had by belief in a master or, more simply, a master's name. It is a wonderful, albeit misperceived, theory. One must have sufficient faith in a master to practice his or her teachings, but it is the practice of these that results in spiritual growth, not passive beliefs in names or anything else. Salvation requires sustained effort and utmost devotion; the soul must come to desire Spirit as single-heartedly as a drowning person craves air. Consider these various scriptural injunctions and the quality of righteous resolve they require:

> Sanctify yourselves therefore, and be ye holy: for I am the Lord your God. And ye shall keep my statutes, and do them: I am the Lord which sanctify you.[14]

> Thou shalt love the Lord thy God with all thy heart, and with all thy soul, and with all thy mind.[15]

> Immerse thy mind in Me alone; concentrate on Me thy discriminative perception; and beyond doubt thou shalt dwell immortally in Me.[16]

> Beneath the banyan bough
> On sacred seat I take this vow;
> "Until life's mystery I solve,
> Until I gain the Priceless Lore,
> Though bones and fleeting flesh dissolve,
> I'll leave this posture nevermore."[17]

Clearly, spiritual attainment is not achieved easily. Years, nay, lives, of dedicated commitment may be required to free ourselves from the taint of delusion. That is why having a spiritual master and correct path to follow are such a blessing; they help expedite the process. In a guru-disciple relationship, the master assumes 25 percent of a disciple's burden and God takes on 50 percent. The remaining 25 percent must be fulfilled by the disciple—and that requires giving one's all. Personal effort is our spiritual responsibility. We must practice righteousness to harvest its fruits.

Having challenged misperceived concepts of receiving a master and belief on a master's name, it is only fair to provide a correct, esoteric interpretation of them. The phrase "to receive" means being able to contain. If we sought to receive the ocean in a cup, it would not be possible. The cup would have to be enlarged so the sea could fit within it. Likewise, no finite mind can hold the divine immensity. Human awareness must be expanded from body identification to cosmic consciousness to receive God. This expansion is achieved by progressive stages of meditation.

"Believing on a name" is another compelling phrase, but it does not infer gaining spiritual growth by passive receptivity. Mice may live on sacred grounds but will not become holy because of mere proximity. Similarly, while honoring a saint's name is respectful, it cannot produce sanctity. Action is needed for outcomes. On an esoteric level to be addressed later, believing on the name of God refers to attunement to the Word of God, the Om or Amen. For our more immediate purposes, "believing" involves a kind of active receptivity: the subtle ability to attract a master's blessings through the principles of vibrational affinity. Vibrations can be imbued with consciousness. Just as turning a radio to certain stations dials in related frequencies, attuning to, or "believing upon," a saint by devotion, right action, and faith forms a conduit through which vibrations from that saint's consciousness are drawn. Consider the biblical story of the woman who "drew" Jesus's healing:

And a woman having an issue of blood twelve years, which had spent all her living upon physicians, neither could be healed of any, came behind him, and touched the border of his garment: and immediately her issue of blood stanched. And Jesus said, Who touched me? When all denied, Peter and they that were with him said, Master, the multitude throng thee and press thee, and sayest thou, Who touched me? And Jesus said, Somebody hath touched me: for I perceive that virtue is gone out of me. And when the woman saw that she was not hid, she came trembling, and falling down before him, she declared unto him before all the people for what cause she had touched him, and how she was healed immediately. And he said unto her, Daughter, be of good comfort: thy faith hath made thee whole; go in peace.[18]

In this instance, the issue of belief, that is, vibratory transmission, was associated with a physical touch, but the principles involved are identical. The woman had sufficient faith in Jesus that a channel of receptivity was opened so that his divine power could flow to and heal her. As Peter noted, Jesus was crowded by numerous people, yet similar incidents had not occurred. It was the woman's profound faith that allowed the sacred exchange to occur.

A less spectacular event validated this phenomenon for me in, of all places, Las Vegas. My wife was attending a medical conference, so I went along for the adventure. Given my sensitivities, however, the tawdry environs soon became burdensome. Determined to counter such influences, I sought refuge in prayerful meditation. While invoking my spiritual lineage, I inexplicably began experiencing waves of relief pass through me, a surprising and unexpected response that increased with every repeated invocation. Evidently, the summoning process aligned my consciousness to the higher vibrational field of my masters and provided me with a personal lesson in the laws of affinity. The truth of believing on a name became glaringly evident as a manifestation of spiritual attunement, yet a clear effort had to be made to receive that grace. Effort and faith must be combined with receptivity to attune one's consciousness to spiritual states and partake of the power therein.

9. *Powers and miracles do not reflect knowledge of God, nor do they impart salvation.*

Years ago, while living in Marin County, California, I attended several bizarre events that left a lasting impression on me. One was a carnival-like affair promoting an allegedly extraordinary spiritual experience. The next was a highly unusual Chamber of Commerce meeting, and the last was a pseudoshamanistic ceremony. In the first instance, I had just come from months of classical yogic and meditation training in an isolated mountain ashram. Curious to see what else could be added to my metaphysical plate, I visited the meeting, which morphed into an amusing snake-oil adventure. As this New Age farce unfolded, a stately white-haired man presented himself to the audience with a sexy blonde female assistant. Declaring that he had attained cosmic consciousness, he offered those present a glimpse into this exalted spiritual state. Of course, it was but a preview. To access the complete experience, one needed to attend his comprehensive workshops. No surprise there. Well, everyone was ushered into a revival-style tent and asked to sit still with eyes closed. Lights were dimmed, gentle music turned on, and gradually a sound-and-light show commenced that soon became a riot of discordant noise and color, a cacophony that allegedly replicated superconscious states of supernal peace, bliss, and expanded awareness. It was a sensory assault, not a supersensory episode. Were I at a night club or restaurant with such racket blaring, I would leave immediately, not pay for more. Yet many in the audience seemed taken by the huckster's pitch and, instead of wincing at its wrongness, were conned into paying hefty workshop fees and felt grateful for that opportunity! After departing, I considered the spectacle a lesson in discernment some would have to learn the hard way: God is not a carnie, and sensory fireworks are no measure of refined attainment.

Following this faux spiritual revival, my next adventure was with the Marin County Chamber of Commerce. In context, mid-1980s Marin County was a center for New Age everything: crystals, channeling, and all manner of psychic frippery. During this meeting, merchants discussed which of their "spirit guides" was deemed the best business advisor. One disembodied entity found particular favor because it promoted a platform of inner growth through opulence. Evidently, the more you had, the less you were shackled by limitation consciousness, thereby demonstrating the unlimited nature and abundance of Spirit. To me, it was just a tidy justification for avarice. When asked my opinion, I shared the following story, loosely adapted from a tale called "The Philosopher's Stone."[19]

Once there was a prince who possessed an alchemist's stone capable of turning anything it touched into gold. While hunting in the forest one day, he fell from his horse, struck his head on a rock, and lost consciousness. An old hermit saw the accident and hastened to the prince's aid. When the prince recovered, he wanted to reward the recluse, so loaned him the stone for a week. The ascetic humbly accepted the magical gift, agreeing to return it seven days hence.

As the week passed, the prince anticipated seeing the recluse residing in a forest of incalculable wealth; where once there had only been twigs, bracken, and leaves, he expected to see glades of gold. When they reunited, however, he was astonished to see the hermit wearing the same tattered robe and staying in the same dilapidated hut. He had not changed a thing. Not meaning to be impolite, the prince exchanged pleasantries until he could not restrain his curiosity any longer and asked why the hermit had not used the stone to improve his conditions. The hermit replied, "Oh, that silly thing? I must have tossed it in the creek." Horrified, the prince leapt into the stream and frantically splashed about, searching for the coveted rock. Smiling, the hermit waded into the stream and gently assured him it was not lost. Saying this, he stooped over and began retrieving stone after stone, using each to turn whatever it touched into gold. Amazed, the prince stuffed the magical horde into his saddlebag and rode off, intoxicated with visions of untold riches.

Early the next morning, however, the prince returned looking haggard and despondent. With twinkling eyes, the hermit asked why he had come and what was troubling him. The prince said that while reveling in his good fortune, he suddenly became wistful. He thought the magic stones offered unshakable security and happiness but soon realized they could be lost or stolen. Furthermore, he might get ill and not be able to enjoy the opulence they provided. Reflecting on these matters, he recalled the recluse's serenity and uncanny ability to create wealth by fashioning similar stones. Deciding he must find such inner peace, even amid poverty, he opted to forsake his wealth and seek training from the saintly recluse. The old man beamed a gentle smile and replied, "My son, you have just taken the first step on the road to wisdom: realizing that nothing material can bestow lasting joy. Now that you are free of that delusion, I will gladly teach you how to transform your mind into a gold mine of eternal happiness."

In retrospect, I suspect my tale was none too popular with the chamber audience. But if money made for or represented spirituality, then Jesus, Moses, Krishna, and Buddha would have been tycoons. But none of them sought such things. Prosperity is not to be denigrated, and money is not evil; it is neutral and can be used for great good or negative ends. However, the idea that riches bestow happiness is a classic delusion born of worldly identification and must be eliminated by wisdom. Nerves are like little tubes through which sensations are conveyed. To identify our happiness with those perceptions is deadly. Our true Self, the soul, is joy and does not depend on sensations or gold for fulfillment.

The last incident I attended was a bizarre ritual that, for lack of a better title, I call a power-animal release ceremony. The event was sponsored by a spiritual healing center and purportedly utilized shamanic techniques to help participants bypass intellectual restraints and access primal feeling. While I bow to the valid use of shamanism to induce heightened states of consciousness and guide one's journey through life, what I experienced was like a trendy, insincere imitation. Base instincts were invoked by a contrived combination of drumming, grunting, and hyperventilation. People were ridiculed for self-control, prompted to emotional abandon, and praised for histrionic, animal-like antics. It was an exercise in emotional indulgence and insulting to genuine shamanism. People can whip themselves into a frenzy, but intense emotional states are not the stuff of spiritual realization. Emotionalism is the unfiltered, distorted side of feeling that views perception through the lens of bias and intoxicating excitation. People in such states may equate their emotions with truth, but that is erroneous self-justification; the two are worlds apart. Truth is the exact correspondence with reality. Impartial feeling, unlike emotionalism, is a mirror that registers and reflects what is placed before it accurately. It manifests the clarity of awareness needed to perceive truth flawlessly. Emotional indulgence, on the other hand, obscures truth by virtue of its tempestuous constitutional incapacity to receive it. Just as a still pond accurately reflects images on its surface, calm feeling can discern truth. Choppy waters, however, like emotionalism, distort similar images and offer little besides the thrill of turbulence.

Since pseudoshamanic themes were incorporated in the program, a word must be said about that. All aspects of creation are manifestations of Spirit and offer invaluable lessons about life. Yet humans hold a rarified place on the evolutionary ladder by virtue of their unique energetic anatomy, the chakra system. It allows us access to states of supreme consciousness that animals cannot have. This statement is not pejorative; it is physiologic fact. Less-evolved creatures are governed chiefly by fight-or-flight limbic systems that most humans advanced past long ago. In short, animalism is not enlightenment; it is primitivistic. Being aware of the lessons God provides through nature is not the same as manifesting the traits or mentalities of less-developed creations. If that were so, then all Taoist sages would be kin to Tarzan. Being attuned with nature means being in harmony with its source, Spirit, not devolving to beastly status.

10. God alone must be the object of worship.

Given an ever-increasing interest in metaphysical matters, it is not surprising that questionable trends arise. Here I refer chiefly to fascination with angels, nature spirits, and astral entities. While such beings exist, and some merit genuine respect, they should not be worshipped. Even reverence toward saints or prophets who act for God should not segue into worshipping them; worship is reserved for God alone. Any deviation from this tenet violates a fundamental spiritual mandate as stated clearly in the first two of the Ten Commandments, foundation of the Abrahamic faiths: "I am the Lord thy God. . . . Thou shalt have no other gods before me. Thou shalt not make unto thee any graven image, or any likeness of any thing that is in heaven above, or that is in the earth beneath, or that is in the water under the earth."[20]

The Bhagavad Gita also addresses proper veneration, albeit from a broad perspective that incorporates saints, avatars, angels, astral deities, and Spirit itself. While this scope includes the subtle realms, God is still the sole one deserving of worship. "Whatever embodiment (a God-incarnate, a saint, or a deity) a devotee strives faithfully to worship, it is I who make his devotion unflinching."[21]

Angels are high beings created to serve God. If one feels inspired by or grateful toward them, that is appropriate, but, in keeping with this theme, God alone is due our homage. The same applies to the forces fashioned by God to guide and sustain creation: nature spirits or astral deities. Here, too, we are enjoined to remain focused on the Creator, not the creation. As for astral beings that claim to be teachers or guides, be wary. Good entities as well as bad exist, and the latter may pose as something they are not to beguile or gain unmerited attention. Disembodiment does not make anyone holy; it is just a function of not having physical form. We do not become angelic just because we pass into an astral realm; after-death consciousness is identical to that possessed while incarnate. Therefore, it is ill advised to consort with astral "guides" or those who purport to represent them. The entities may be of questionable intent, and it is difficult to discern whether the messages conveyed are authentic or merely the subconscious projections of those giving them. Besides, sanctified teachers who lived on earth leave enduring legacies through written or demonstrated teachings. Their works need not be updated via channeled postscripts, nor will they submit to random invocation. If the divine aid of saints is desired, one must access it directly through traditional means of fasting, prayer, and meditation, not through mediums. Steer clear of curious phenomena and worship God alone.

11. Eight classic attributes of God are light, sound, wisdom, power, love, peace, calmness, and joy.

While infinite in expression, Spirit has eight eternal attributes evident throughout creation. Being present in our souls, they provide the means to access Spirit directly within or to demonstrate divine qualities in daily life.

Light and sound are the initial vibratory expressions of transcendental Spirit arising at creation's inception. They are the primal, foundational building blocks out of which the rest of manifestation is assembled. In Taoist terms, the conjuring of existence from a seeming void is expressed in the following verse: "Non-existence is called the antecedent of heaven and earth; Existence is the mother of all things. From eternal non-existence, therefore, we serenely observe the mysterious beginning of the Universe."[22]

In classical Western context, the sound element is depicted as the Word of God. "In the beginning was the word, and the word was with God."[23]

In due course, we shall learn how significant the Word aspect becomes with regard to certain meditation practices.

Wisdom refers to the right use of intuitional discernment that allows one to live in perfect alignment with universal truth and cosmic law. Paramahansa Yogananda said, "Sorrow, illness, and failure are natural results of transgressions against God's laws. Wisdom consists in avoiding such violations and finding peace and happiness within yourself through thoughts and actions that are in harmony with your real Self."[24] Avoiding wrong actions and adhering to right ones also implies the ability to choose correctly between the two. Doing so successfully and living accordingly is wisdom.

Power is the aspect of Spirit that keeps the universe operational. On an individual level, certain practices can tap cosmic power to increase vitality and, if channeled correctly, enhance spiritual growth. Although it is also possible to develop paranormal capabilities through specific exercises, such skills are not to be pursued for their own sake. Unusual powers, like a flower's fragrance, may arise as we blossom spiritually, but these are natural by-products of inner realization, not goals of themselves.

Love is the all-in-all of Spirit. It is harmony. It is law. It nurtures and unites all things. It is an actual force and power, the essence of Being, whose magnetism draws everything back unto itself. It is the thread out of which the universe is woven, that which we all crave, and the sole thing God wants from us. No progress on the spiritual path can be made without love. Saint Augustine commented, "You have made us for yourself, O Lord, and our heart is restless until it rests in you."[25] And it is so. When we surrender ourselves completely, in love, to That Which Is Love, the barriers of separation between soul and Spirit dissolve, and final liberation is but an act of grace away.

Peace is the precursor to calm and a state in which all vibrations, positive or negative, are stilled. When one enters meditative silence, the experience arising from stopping mental excitation is peace. It is an emptiness resulting from the absence of stimuli. While denoting a mind clear of distraction, it has limited shelf life, so to speak. Were we to stay in its negative zone overly long, we would become bored by the intrinsic vacuum. Diving deeper into peace, however, produces a self-sustaining positive condition "which passeth all understanding."[26] That is calmness. One can abide in calmness endlessly, for it has an independent existence and is enjoyable in and of itself.

Joy is the bliss nature of Spirit. Progressive meditation takes us beyond peace and calmness to ever-deepening levels of unconditional joy. Of joy, Sri Yukteswar, Yogananda's guru, said, "Spiritual advancement is not to be measured by one's display of outward powers but solely by the depth of his bliss in meditation.... Desire for material things is endless; man is never satisfied completely, and pursues one goal after another. The 'something else' he seeks is the Lord, who alone can grant lasting joy."[27] In this context, even love is not the highest goal of spiritual practice. That place is reserved for joy. We seek love for many reasons, but, ultimately, what beckons us is the unending joy it imparts.

In light of these qualities and the omnipotent omnipresence of God, many people wonder why evil exists. I offer one simple perspective: Evil exists in a relative context only; in an absolute sense, it does not exist. In divine consciousness, all things emanate from the eternal source, which, of itself, *is* infinite goodness. Cosmic contrasts are vital for creation to unfold. Without opposites, everything would be uniform. Accordingly, lacking a shadow, we could not discern the light. Such delineations of duality disturb us when we suffer. That is understandable. Yet beneath the turmoil of cosmic diversity is the all-benevolent, unified eternity. With wisdom, we eventually learn to see beyond the ever-changing veils of nature and anchor ourselves in the enduring contentment of the soul. "Only those who take shelter in Me (the Cosmic Hypnotizer) become free from this power of illusion."[28] Lest I be misunderstood, none of this implies that evil does not exist. It does. There are cosmic forces that perpetuate evil thoughts and deeds. Yet even these are subject to the One and, arguably, are instruments of the cosmic drama. That is small comfort in the face of hardship but is, I believe, the truth.

12. Spiritual progress, though subtle, is measurable in definite ways.

Modern society thrives on results, and Western culture wants things quickly and easily. Sadly, this attitude has infected many on the spiritual path. Beginners often desire high states of consciousness as if they were products available at a convenience store. Assessing progress is viable if it reinforces wholesome efforts but deleterious if it encourages goal fixation or dangerous fast-track efforts. The manifestation of divine consciousness takes time and cannot be rushed. Subtle astral channels must be purified and strengthened to handle potent energy surges. Without this preparation, superabundant vital forces would fry ill-prepared nervous systems. Spiritual zeal and unrestrained striving paradoxically increase tension and egocentrism. They must be tempered by humility, patience, and devotion. Calm enthusiasm facilitates the balanced receptivity needed to elicit positive results.

Soul awakening is subtle and challenging to gauge. Paranormal talents are not valid indicators so much as is increasing love of God, joy, peace, kindness, wisdom, compassion, and harmony with others. Daily reflection reveals whether positive or negative traits rule our inner kingdom and life activities.

A reliable list of measures for spiritual development includes:

- Increasing peacefulness during meditation

- Conscious experience of calmness in meditation changing into increasing bliss

- Deeper understanding and the receiving of answers by intuition

- Increasing mental and physical efficiency

- Love for meditation and preference for its peace and joy over worldly allures

- Expanding sense of equal and unconditional love for all

- True worship of and contact with God as increasing, ever-new bliss in meditation, creation, and beyond

CHAPTER 5

I encourage readers to review these twelve principles periodically to enrich their understanding. Repeated exposure to important topics is central to growth and retention. As we evolve, we are able to detect nuances or insights that previously were less apparent or simply did not register.

The next two chapters target ten essential attitudes and behaviors necessary for inner awakening. They are the cornerstones of spiritual training. Although soul growth is a delicate thing to measure, these attributes, when perfected, demonstrate proof of soul maturity.

6

Right Behavior: Guidelines for Thought and Deed, Part One

The Don'ts

Folk wisdom says that attitude is everything. While not completely so, it is true that perceptions are powerful. They contribute to interactions with others by shaping views and eliciting corresponding reactions. Behaviors and responses perpetuate cyclic patterns of engagement. If attitudes are wise, this scenario is fine; however, if not, it bodes ill. In this chapter, a code of conduct—actions and attitudes—is discussed that, being rooted in universal divine law, fosters spiritual growth and harmony.

Central to this code is the underlying principle that creation's multiplicity is a manifestation of one substance, Spirit. Thoughts and deeds that spring from this understanding promote growth and inner attainment. Oppositional responses perpetuate delusion and impede development. To awaken spiritually, we must embrace the reality of divine unity, not because of blind doctrine but because it is true. Correspondingly, we must forsake everything that endorses separateness from God. The code distills the art of perfect living into ten guidelines, five of which will be addressed in this chapter and five in the next. Why do I say "perfect

CHAPTER 6

living"? Because the practices outlined reflect expressions of soul consciousness, not mere sociological imperatives. They teach us how to live
as beings of pure Spirit while physically incarnate. Very simply, the code
fosters the goal of life itself: illumination and freedom from delusion.
Let's review the components collectively and then examine each
individually.

Code of Illumination

Ten Qualities of Self-Control in Thought and Deed

(Based on Patanjali's Eight-Limbed Path)

Don'ts	Dos
Nonviolence	Devotion to Spirit
Nonlying	Self-study
Nonstealing	Contentment
Nonsensuality	Cleanliness
Nongreed	Austerity

It is evident that the five elements in the left column are preceded by the
prefix *non*. The rationale for this is that they stress refraining from
thoughts and/or deeds contributing to deluded states of consciousness.
The implication is that the soul is innately perfect and that by abstaining
from wrongdoing, righteousness and purified awareness manifest naturally. For instance, by removing violence from our consciousness, harmony will emerge automatically. Similarly, by erasing greed, we gain
contentment. Again, mastery of these disciplines cultivates an illumined
consciousness because it replaces misleading mindsets with divinely
attuned ones.

NONVIOLENCE

In the presence of one firmly established in non-violence, all hostilities cease.
—Patanjali, *Yoga Sutras* 2:35[1]

Nonviolence, like all elements in this code, must be understood and applied in the context of our body/mind/spirit nature. The spiritual part, however, is most important and drives the other aspects.

Physical Application

No one would argue that refraining from physical violence is a bad thing, if only to maintain social order. However, nonviolence needs to be evaluated more insightfully. Life, human or other, comes from Spirit and is not something we have the power to give or take. We share in but do not possess life. Though we kill to eat (preferably fruits and vegetables) or destroy germs for health's sake, we seldom have just cause to inflict injury or end life unless for self-defense. Life exists to evolve and manifest the consciousness of God. By abstaining from physical violence, we affirm our intrinsic kinship with all existence and act in ways that honor this reality.

Mental Application

Applied mentally, nonviolence becomes increasingly subtle. It forbids thinking ill of others, or even wishing them harm. Critical thoughts actually create inner discord more hurtful to us than to those we judge. Thought is a powerful force. Mental hostility precipitates nervous agitation, increased blood pressure, and a compromised immune system. Psychologically, we become aggressive, defensive, and temperamentally repellant. The more we rail at others, the more our constitutional balance is disturbed. While these reasons to forego mental violence are self-serving, they inadvertently teach proper behavior by prodding us toward right attitudes and acts. As the desire to harm is released from our consciousness, a compassionate regard for others emerges like a sweet fragrance previously overshadowed by noxious odors. The soul's innate harmony becomes increasingly manifest as we allow it mental expression. Accordingly, it evinces the optimal conditions by which inner and outer peace can flourish.

In such a mind, a violent thought cannot arise, let alone a hostile word or deed.

Nonviolence is the law of the human race and is infinitely greater than and superior to brute force. . . . When nonviolence is accepted as the law of life, it must pervade the whole being and not be applied to isolated acts.[2]

[Ahimsa, noninjury] stands at the center of the nonviolent discipline. . . . You are constantly moving to the point where you love your enemy. . . . It is an overflowing love which seeks nothing in return. Theologians would say that it is love of God operating in the human heart.[3]

You have heard that it was said, You shall love your neighbor and hate your enemy; But I say to you, Love your enemies and pray for those whose persecute you, so that you may be children of your Father in heaven; for he makes his sun rise on the evil and on the good, and sends rain on the righteous and on the unrighteous. For if you love those who love you, what reward do you have?[4]

Spiritual Application

This aspect of nonviolence is summed up by the widely paraphrased Golden Rule: Do unto others as you would have done unto you. Everyone is part of your cosmic Self. What you do to others in thought or deed you do to your larger universal Self. The idea that one can cause hurt without effecting repercussion reinforces delusional separation from life and God; it erects walls of self-created isolation that deny the truth that Spirit abides in all. Such actions are destined to create miserable lives of bitter estrangement. For example, I knew someone whose vindictive grudges resulted in her being completely alienated from family and friends at the time of her death, a situation that, sadly, is not unique. In the final analysis, those who dispense violent thinking and behavior pay for it the most.

Perfected nonviolence manifests perfect harmony. In its highest form, nonviolence generates an aura of peace that eliminates the harmful inclinations of all beings—animal or human—that come within its energetic field. Saint Francis demonstrated this spiritual state by preaching to rapt audiences of birds and mollifying a vicious wolf. Various Hindu legends tell of reclusive saints who affectionately shared their forest habitats with wild tigers and cobras. Nonviolence creates a magnetism of attraction and peaceable harmony because vibrational elements of division and dissonance are replaced by those of loving, divine unity.

Affirmations of truth are a way of tuning in with the divine cosmic vibration. They can be used to promote vibrational healing or to fashion specific attitudes and behaviors. Accordingly, I have included one or more affirmative phrases after each quality. Repeat these affirmations, or ones like them, upon waking or going to sleep to promote nonviolence or any quality associated with this code. These seed thoughts will sink deep into the receptive soil of the subconscious if repeated faithfully over time and, if not corroded by doubt, will stimulate positive shifts in perception, action, and experience. Miraculous results can occur when affirmations go sufficiently deep to touch the superconscious mind. Here is an affirmation to use for cultivating an attitude of nonviolence:

As a child of God, all creation is part of my divine Self.

I radiate peace and harmony, love and goodwill to all.

NONLYING

As truthfulness is achieved, the fruits of actions naturally result according to the will of the yogi.
> —Patanjali, *Yoga Sutras*, 2:36[5]

The second element in this code is nonlying, sometimes referred to as truthfulness. More than just a matter of not telling falsehoods, it is abstaining from self-deception. This practice is important because accurate perceptions of reality come partly from the absence of wishful thinking. Truth is not a matter of personal belief or bias; it is the exact correspondence with reality. In the crucible of nonlying, we remove false layers of ego that perpetuate delusion in order to discern our true identity as soul. Mahatma Gandhi was famous for a selfless adherence to truth. These quotations reflect his devotion to this principle:

Search for Truth is search for God. Truth is God. God is because Truth is.[6]

Truth is by nature self-evident. As soon as you remove the cobwebs of ignorance that surround it, it shines clear.[7]

Physical Application

Practicing nonlying can be complex since facts do not always reflect truth. For example, after failing a relatively easy test, it is not uncommon to feel bad or perhaps label oneself as stupid. In reality, though, the soul is omniscient; ignorance is just part of the undeveloped ego. By identifying with mistakes, we reinforce delusion; by affirming our soul potential, we invoke its actuality. This statement is not meant to endorse denial or avoid self-improvement, but to help us look beyond immediate errors to what is eternal. Consider how children are expected to make mistakes as they grow. Our job is not to blame them, but to guide their understanding so they can eventually govern themselves wisely. In the context of nonlying, self-awareness must be applied nonjudgmentally to uproot and move past limitations.

In social situations, nonlying can require tricky maneuvering. It is easy to hurt people through bluntness, and doing so is often senselessly cruel. Revealing another's flaws seldom accomplishes much other than to make ourselves seem superior. Such exposure is not only unkind but unnecessary unless needed to correct a grave injustice. This brand of "honesty" is actually more akin to hypocritical gossip that opposes nonviolence. It invigorates those who like causing pain and may erode another's will to reform. In such circumstances, it is best to remain quiet or, to paraphrase scripture, to focus on removing the mote from one's own eye before denouncing another. Conversely, telling white lies to protect someone creates a slippery moral slope, as does not speaking up when truth should be told. In circumstances where sparing another's feelings is appropriate, remain silent or consider gentle words delivered kindly. Critical details and hard truths may be unavoidable when serious stakes are at play. Even then, nonlying must be blended with nonviolence to produce an expression of truthfulness beneficial to all. In the final analysis, truth is a positive force, an uplifting, encouraging panacea, not a faultfinding exposé of questionably relevant facts.

Mental Application

Fortunately, human ignorance and ideological folly do not impact Spirit. "For my thoughts are not your thoughts, neither are your ways my ways, saith the Lord."[8]

What we believe or want to be true may not be so. As indicated earlier, a nonlying mindset is needed to vigilantly spot and eliminate delusion wherever it arises within us or, if applicable, in others. A classic case of admonishing falseness was expressed when Jesus chided Peter for being delusion's mouthpiece: "But he turned, and said unto Peter, 'Get thee behind me, Satan: thou art an offence unto me: for thou savourest not the things that be of God, but those that be of men.'"[9] People commonly claim "I'm only human" to justify incompetence, as if humanity is a species of innate bunglers. We can and often do underachieve, but being human is not a pseudonym for ineptitude. The truth is that Spirit abides in all; by dedicated effort, we can transmute ego flaws into expressions of perfect divine will and accomplishment. In fact, nonlying insists that we actualize our innate greatness. A famous passage by Marianne Williamson eloquently invites us to embrace our power and potential:

> Our deepest fear is not that we are inadequate. Our deepest fear is that we are powerful beyond measure. It is our light, not our darkness that most frightens us. We ask ourselves, Who am I to be brilliant, gorgeous, talented, fabulous? Actually, who are you *not* to be? You are a child of God. Your playing small does not serve the world. There is nothing enlightened about shrinking so that other people won't feel insecure around you. We are all meant to shine, as children do. We were born to make manifest the glory of God that is within us. It's not just in some of us; it's in everyone. And as we let our own light shine, we unconsciously give other people permission to do the same. As we are liberated from our own fear, our presence automatically liberates others.[10]

Nonlying requires accepting our true nature. Mistakes and gains do not define us. If you fall, get up. Correct yourself. Error is but a temporary blip on the evolutionary screen. As children of Spirit, we are eternal and divine. Knowing this helps us remain balanced and cheerful amid the tempests of life.

The following meditative visualization helps you identify more fully with your eternal nature:

> Sit comfortably and close your eyes.
>
> Visualize yourself floating on a sea of light. Silently feel Spirit within and around you, above and below you, in front and behind, on your left and on your right.
>
> Imagine Spirit as the light that fashioned the universe and you. Sense it in your blood, bones, muscles, cells, and thoughts. Realize there is no place that Spirit is not.
>
> Relax and affirm, *"Spirit and I are one!"* and melt expansively into this light.

Spiritual Application

This aspect of nonlying gives rise to two significant realizations. First, Spirit is at the core of our being. It is the universal activating power, the only good and sole accomplisher of all.

> I seek not mine own will, but the will of the Father which hath sent me.[11]

> I am the Ultimate Goal, the Upholder, the Master, the Witness, the Shelter, the Refuge, and the One Friend. I am the Origin, the Dissolution, the Foundation, the Cosmic Storehouse, and the Seed Indestructible.[12]

Reflection here reveals that all power to reason, will, and act comes from God. It is not that we lack capabilities, but that ours are on loan from the Infinite. To live a spiritual life, we must exercise our divinely bestowed gifts in alignment with divine will: By doing so, we harness the power of Spirit for all-around success.

The second realization is that truth has vibrational qualities attuned to creation. When nonlying is perfected, words and thoughts gain materializing power.

The will of masters united to God and in tune with Christ consciousness is charged with creative power. All such great ones can perform miracles through thought, word, or deed if divinely directed. In *Autobiography of a Yogi*, Yogananda writes that his guru, Sri Yukteswar, told him that his guru, Lahiri Mahasaya, was a master who healed many persons in seemingly curious ways. Once he healed Yukteswar by simply stating, "It [a state of perfect health] is so, even at this moment." When asked how this state could be achieved, the master simply stated, "Thought is a force, even as electricity or gravitation. The human mind is a spark of the almighty consciousness of God." Yukteswar clarified, "My guru, awake in God, knew this world to be nothing but an objectivized dream of the Creator. Because he was completely aware of his unity with the Divine Dreamer, Lahiri Mahasaya could materialize or dematerialize or make any other change he wished in the dream atoms of the phenomenal world."[13]

Such is the consummate proof and by-product of perfected nonlying; what we speak becomes reality. The following affirmation is useful in developing this virtue:

My thoughts, words, and deeds are in perfect harmony with the divine will that flows through me.

NONSTEALING

To one established in nonstealing, all wealth comes.
—Patanjali, *Yoga Sutras* 2:37

This third quality forbids theft of material items and intangible qualities such as honor, affection, praise, or fame. Even law courts recognize alienation of affection as a crime arising from the theft of love or relationship. So thievery is wrong regardless of how subtle the desired object is.

Physical Application

According to karmic law, if you earn something, it will come unbidden. Accepting this principle lets us remain content and confident in the immaculate fairness of God. Early in life I realized that my career pursuits were essentially selfish and shortsighted. Like many people, I wanted what I wanted without concern for larger issues. Eventually seeing the error of my ways, I learned to replace self-favoring desires with whatever might benefit the greater good. With this shift I realized that I could get whatever job was meant for me and for which I did my utmost to qualify. If unsuccessful in a particular pursuit, I should gracefully accept the fact and let it go. This perspective may also be applied to attracting mates, homes—anything we wish. Such beliefs may seem contrary to healthy ambition, but that is not so. We should heed heartfelt aspirations and do our best to realize them, yet relinquish attachment to outcomes. This point is aptly put in the Bhagavad Gita: "Surrender unto My will with subdued mind, and renounce [the attachment to, and the anxiety for] the fruits of all work [by learning to accept all results as God-given, with equanimity]."[14] By giving our all in any situation and surrendering the fruits of actions to God, we gain freedom from worry, coupled with assurance of merited divine aid. A spiritual life requires trusting Spirit to hold the best for us in all circumstances at all times. We may not always understand the big picture when things are hard or do not work out as we prefer, but we can, and should, have faith in the process. Remember that the universe does not operate randomly, but by immutable law, and is designed to help us grow in wisdom and joy. Such recognition helps us practice nonstealing by accepting what we already possess with equanimity and realizing that true happiness cannot be found in things. This is not a passive ideology but one that supports earnest effort coupled with discernment and surrender. To underscore that point, know that we are never trapped by fate. God will help those willing to help themselves if their dreams are not satisfied. There is nothing wrong with ambition; there is merely the need to exercise it ethically and with right attitude.

Mental/Emotional Application

Stealing indicates a direction of consciousness away from Spirit. By its very nature, it implies a disconnection from innate wholeness, a suggestion that things outside the Self—tangible or otherwise—produce joy and that happiness can be gained through acquisitions. Worldly consciousness pursues externals in a relentless search for fulfillment. Nonstealing opposes this outward-flowing delusion by emphasizing that material elements can never gratify the soul. What we actually crave is found by turning to the endless bliss of Spirit within the sanctuary of the Self. "Whosoever drinketh of this water [materiality] shall thirst again: But whosoever drinketh of the water that I shall give him [Spirit] shall never thirst [crave happiness through sensory pursuit]."[15] On a related note, it is not unusual for people to seek emotional fulfillment by indulging in food, work, sex, drink, and so forth. Semiaddictive behaviors are not stealing per se but share kindred subconscious drives to counter inner emptiness through external gratification. As this mindset is similar to that of stealing, so is its remedy: seek happiness from within.

By way of example, I once counseled a friend after his lover left that her presence had become not just a factor of his happiness and sense of worth but a condition for it. When I saw him next, he was upbeat and enjoyably engaged in new adventures. Reflecting on our session, he realized that lovers were definitely welcome in his life but not essential to his core well-being. Bravo to my friend! It was a hard lesson to learn, yet it freed him from a common dependency pattern. When this motif is applied to nonstealing, it becomes apparent that no thing, tangible or otherwise, gives joy. Inclinations to grab fulfillment externally simply fall away.

Spiritual Application

Nonstealing reinforces faith in a benevolent and responsive universe. What is rightly ours will always come without force or illicit pursuit. In fact, perfection of this virtue is said to manifest a highly practical outcome: One's needs are met without having to ask for them. Nonstealing also heightens appreciation of life by freeing the soul from material dependence; we learn to enjoy things fully without the weight of desire. If that seems unusual, consider visiting a zoo, where marvelous creatures are seen, without any corresponding need to own them. The key here lies in understanding that nonattachment is not indifference; it produces enthusiasm untainted by craving. And nonstealing is more than an absence of criminal acts. Being anchored in contentment eliminates the tendency to be ensnared by false glamour or wrong thinking and makes harboring ill-gotten gains unconscionable.

A touching story I like to share about nonstealing involves a young girl I knew. She was brought to Chicago by train on her birthday to visit her aunt. She arrived in the morning and spent the day sightseeing with her grandmother, aunt, uncle, and me. At dinner, we all went to a quaint Italian restaurant, which was lovely but mostly empty. Noticing she had no same-age playmates, I offered a sympathetic prayer on her behalf. It just did not seem right that she suffer through her birthday dinner with a bunch of old fogies! Not long afterward, a rather amazing thing occurred: the doors opened and in streamed various friends and relatives of the restaurant owners. Soon the place was packed with animated Italians and, of course, tons of kids. Just then, we gave the secret signal and the girl's birthday cake was brought out with candles blazing and waiters singing. All the newly arrived young ones rushed over in an uninhibited desire to see, and have, some cake. Fortunately, it was large enough to share, and the girl was thrilled by this impromptu gala. While all this was happening, I slipped over to the jukebox and noticed "Happy Birthday" on the song list—something I had never seen on a jukebox before! Naturally I played the song, which added a classical dimension to the event. Mostly, though, I was touched by the display of divine thoughtfulness. Evidently Spirit agreed that the girl should have other children to play and celebrate with on her special day.

This tale demonstrates how nonstealing works; by doing our part and trusting in God to meet our needs (sometimes asking for things is just fine), we are often granted better outcomes than we could have anticipated or prepared ourselves.

I am joyful and complete within my Self.

The universe provides me what I need at the time I need it.

NONSENSUALITY

By one established in continence, vigor is gained.
—Patanjali, *Yoga Sutras* 2:38

Fourth in the code is nonsensuality, which, frankly, is a challenging area to discuss in our sex-fixated culture. Understood correctly, nonsensuality is not nonsexuality, but addresses the avoidance of anything that detracts from being centered in Spirit. We have seen this theme raised in all aspects of the code, and here is no different, merely a matter of specificity. The crux of the matter is this: Where energy is prevalent, so is consciousness, or, as similarly stated in the Bible, "For where your treasure is, there will your heart be also."[16] Energy must be directed within and raised to centers of divine perception in the brain for spiritual growth to flourish. Left to its natural course, energy flows out through sensory nerves to engage the world, and, as pleasurable feelings are enjoyable, we tend to overindulge in whatever causes them. This excess includes all sensations, not just sexual ones. To guard against dissipating tendencies and addictive attachments, nonsensuality promotes conscious use of energy to appreciate and learn from the world without being ensnared or deluded by it. The senses are certainly not bad of themselves, but identifying with the feelings they cause and considering these a source of completion definitely causes problems.

Physical Application

A classic theme in the spiritual arena is that everyone seeks happiness and avoidance of pain. As just mentioned, favorable sensations are often, and unfortunately, mistaken for inner joy. Like the Siren calls of Homeric lore, these misperceptions are seductive, misleading, and destructive if pursued. They obscure realization of subtle realities and perpetuate discontent because consciousness identifies with its perceptions unless inoculated by wisdom. When ignorance reigns, the senses and energy routed through them are misused to pursue fulfillment externally. Evanescent thrills and cravings are sought, which in turn perpetuate disillusionment and cyclic reincarnation. Insight born of pain, sorrow, or wise discernment eventually reveals that such experiences cannot replace the spiritual unity we really seek.

Since Spirit alone brings lasting joy—because it is joy—consciousness must be directed to the centers of divine perception within our subtle anatomy. When done correctly, we find that inner bliss is far more appealing than sensory stimulation. Pursuing the latter becomes like drinking salt water to quench thirst; intended to satisfy cravings, it only increases them. In a corrosive spiral, the more we chase outer gratification, the more we deplete energy and sink into dissatisfaction. The greater our self-control, however, the more we can enjoy the world from a balanced state. Again, nonsensuality is not nonsexuality. Sex has a genuine place in the scheme of things. Nor does nonsensuality oppose using sense faculties rightly. It is but a shield against the false hope for lasting happiness that sense lures induce.

Mental/Emotional Application

Healthy self-esteem is chiefly wrought by cultivating admirable qualities and accomplishments, not by comparing ourselves to others. There will always be individuals more capable than we are, so it is vital not to gauge innate worth by such standards. In a spiritual sense, real success is based on capacity to love, willingness to serve, and Self-realization. By these measures, a poor person filled with divine insight and joy is infinitely better off than a wealthy malcontent. Each of us is already complete in Spirit. Identifying ourselves with the world obscures that essential reality. This realization was demonstrated in a legendary encounter between Alexander the Great and Dandamis, an Indian sage who expressed non-sensuality in a poetically literal manner. Having heard of the sage, Alexander was curious to learn more about him.

> Onesikratês was therefore dispatched to fetch him, and when he found the great sage he said, "Hail to thee, thou teacher of the Brahmins. The son of the mighty god Zeus, King Alexander, who is the sovereign lord of all men, asks you to go to him, and if you comply, he will reward you with great and splendid gifts, but if you refuse will cut off your head."
>
> Dandamis, with a complacent smile, heard him to the end, but did not so much as lift up his head from his couch of leaves, and

while still retaining his recumbent attitude returned this scornful answer:—

"God, the supreme king, is never the author of insolent wrong, but is the creator of light, of peace, of life, of water, of the body of man, and of souls, and these he receives when death sets them free, being in no way subject to evil desire. He alone is the god of my homage, who abhors slaughter and instigates no wars.

"But Alexander is not God, since he must taste of death, and how can such as he be the world's master, who has not yet reached the further shore of the river Tiberoboas, and has not yet seated himself on a throne of universal dominion? Moreover, Alexander has neither as yet entered living into Hades, nor does he know the course of the sun through the central regions of the earth, while the nations on its boundaries have not so much as heard his name.

"If his present dominions are not capacious enough for his desire, let him cross the Ganges River, and he will find a region able to sustain men if the country on our side be too narrow to hold him.

"Know this, however, that what Alexander offers me, and the gifts he promises, are all things to me utterly useless; but the things which I prize, and find of real use and worth, are these leaves which are my house, these blooming plants which supply me with dainty food, and the water which is my drink, while all other possessions and things, which are amassed with anxious care, are wont to prove ruinous to those who amass them, and cause only sorrow and vexation, with which every poor mortal is fully fraught. But as for me, I lie upon the forest leaves, and, having nothing which requires guarding, close my eyes in tranquil slumber; whereas had I gold to guard, that would banish sleep. The earth supplies me with everything, even as a mother her child with milk. I go wherever I please, and there are no cares with which I am forced to cumber myself, against my will.

"Should Alexander cut off my head, he cannot also destroy my soul. My head alone, now silent, will remain, but the soul will go away to its Master, leaving the body like a torn garment upon the earth, whence also it was taken. I then, becoming spirit, shall ascend to my God, who enclosed us in flesh, and left us upon the earth to prove whether when here below we shall prove obedient to his ordinances, and who also will require of us, when we depart hence to his presence, an account of our life, since he is judge of all proud wrong-doing; for the groans of the oppressed become the punishments of the oppressors.

"Let Alexander, then, terrify with these threats those who wish for gold and for wealth, and who dread death, for against us these weapons are both alike powerless, since the Brahmins neither love gold nor fear death. Go, then, and tell Alexander this: 'Dandamis has no need of aught that is yours, and therefore will not go to you, but if you want anything from Dandamis come you to him.'"

Alexander, on receiving from Onesikratês a report of the interview, felt a stronger desire than ever to see Dandamis, who, though old and naked, was the only antagonist in whom he, the conqueror of many nations, had found more than his match.[17]

Nonsensuality, then, is a shield against wrong measures of self-worth and misplaced striving. It keeps us ever mindful of our true nature and that which is of genuine merit: the soul and Spirit.

Spiritual Application

We are hardwired for sensory perception. Ironically, what we are not—a body—is readily apparent to the senses, while what we are—a soul—must be perceived intuitively. Overcoming the sensory mirage is done through wisdom, persistence, and right awareness. Sensory traps embroil us mostly because we lack discernment. Ask yourself whether gratification truly exists externally or whether it is based upon reactions.

Circumstances confuse us because we associate responsive feelings with whatever caused them. Feelings are subjective: What may be exquisite to one is anathema for another. Therefore, joy is not intrinsic to things or people but a reaction to them. Further, the capacity to feel joy arises from its preexistence in our soul. If we did not have joy within, we could not experience it through external triggers. Knowing this lets us use emotional reactions wisely to identify more fully with our spiritual nature. Doing so does not eliminate the capacity to feel, but facilitates the ability to distinguish genuine soul happiness from the experiences that appear to elicit it. By discrimination and meditative discipline, an awareness can be cultivated that defuses sense addictions and illusions of completeness. Through nonsensuality, then, we find completion within, yet can fully appreciate the senses and what they reveal without being entangled by such.

The following anecdote depicts an earthy lesson about nonsensuality. During my yoga training, I, like most men, was no stranger to abundant sexual desire. It seemed inconceivable to me that anyone could be happy without having such drives fulfilled. Confused by classical aspects of nonsensuality that encourage sexual moderation or celibacy, I prayed for greater understanding. That night I dreamt that the lower half of my body was freed of carnal appetites while my heart was filled to overflowing with love. I subsequently learned that sex urges are concentrations of life force that can be transmuted into far more enjoyable states by raising energy from lower chakras to those of higher orientation. Although the impetus to raise energy does not apply just to sexual matters, transmuting related forces to accelerate inner growth is a viable expression of spiritual dedication. This transmutation is the real purpose behind celibacy: allocating vital resources to gain desired ends. If such a course is undertaken, however, it needs to be done in a balanced, nonsuppressive manner lest repression cause psychological distress or abuse issues.

The point of nonsensuality is that souls are made of joy and do not need external stimuli for fulfillment. Sense impressions that bind the consciousness to the body block its ascension to heights of beatitude.

Thus hedonism of any sort, sexual or otherwise, paradoxically sabotages the fulfillment it seeks. Once soul awareness is experienced, a basis for comparison arises that makes releasing sense fixations easier, even desirable. And when nonsensuality is perfected, extraordinary physical, mental, and spiritual vigor manifests, which lends tremendous force to any chosen endeavor. The following affirmation helps cultivate an attitude of nonsensuality:

The senses serve me, not I them. My mind abides in everlasting soul joy.

Nongreed

When nongreed is confirmed, a thorough illumination
of the how and why of one's birth comes.
—Patanjali *Yoga Sutras* 2:39

The element of nongreed differs from nonstealing in that the latter rejects all manner of theft whereas nongreed emphasizes freedom from attachment. Both refute concepts of joy acquired outside the Self and maintain that being Spirit-centered lets one appreciate all things—ours or others—without looking to them for essential completion.

Physical Application

Greed clouds happiness by promoting notions of fulfillment through acquisition. It fuels desire that continually increases cravings like an addictive drug. When we bond to our fixations and associate feelings of gladness with them, the more we have, the more we want. Brief episodes of satiety pass, and we again become riddled with desire in a cycle of perpetual appetite. Greed entices, and attachments, whether toward people or things, bind. Cords of limitation woven with threads of false identification and jealous insecurity taint otherwise impartial states of ownership. Nongreed counters this condition by adamantly asserting freedom, not being defined or possessed by possessions. Rightly understood, whatever we have is on loan from the universe; nothing and no one is intrinsically ours. We can appreciate objects or people and tend them responsibly without succumbing to a faux glamour. Again, it is not wrong to enjoy what we have or to feel loss. Nongreed does not countenance heartlessness. It is mistaken, though, to be emotionally ensnared by anything material or to expect lasting gratification from such. Like all code qualities, nongreed reminds us that contentment is a preexisting condition found within. We are not our possessions nor do they complete us; only God can do that.

Mental Application

Engagement with the world is innately mental. We build lives around likes, dislikes, and ideas of what it takes to be happy. As already indicated, nongreed shatters tendencies to associate ourselves with what we have. Only through liberating nonattachment can the soul experience and express its innate blessedness.

Applications of nongreed on a mental level are numerous. A very beneficial one is unwillingness to let illness dictate attitude. A personal friend was twice diagnosed with breast cancer. Despite the need for either a bilateral mastectomy or chemotherapy and radiation, she remained adamant in her commitment of gratitude toward God. If I had not observed her directly, I might have suspected that her attitude was a sham response, exchanging grief for high-minded denial. It was genuine. She was not thrilled with the situation, but realized her true home was in Spirit and was not going to compromise her faith because of a physical condition. This perspective let her separate the disease from her intrinsic well-being. An admirable attitude and person!

A less dramatic but eminently practical expression of nongreed counters codependence by promoting relationships based on quality measures, not on fear, obligation, or other binding factors. Nongreed builds confidence to navigate life with grace, flexibility, and the capacity to meet whatever unfolds in appropriate ways. If relationships no longer sustain us, we can release them and move forward without chilling constraints. Again, this practice is not a call to heartlessness but the expression of wisdom born of pure feeling, not confused emotion.

Spiritual Application

In its subtlest application, nongreed quickens spiritual liberation by fostering ego-neutralizing dispassion. When associations with body and personality recede—not from psychosis or imbalance but by transcending ego in superconscious meditation—past-life memories emerge to reveal previously hidden aspects of our soul's journey. These insights result from perfect nonattachment, and, while not spiritually significant per se, they provide direct nonintellectual validation of our eternal nature. The following affirmation helps cultivate an attitude of nongreed:

I am not the body, nor the mind. All joy exists
within my eternal Self. I am free!

7

Right Behavior: Guidelines for Thought and Deed, Part Two

The Dos

Code of Illumination

Don'ts	Dos
Nonviolence	Devotion to Spirit
Nonlying	Self-study
Nonstealing	Contentment
Nonsensuality	Cleanliness
Nongreed	Austerity

The Code of Illumination has but one goal: to overcome delusion and elicit soul realization. The five forms of disciplined constraint, the "non" qualities described thus far, stressed what not to do so the Self may manifest its natural virtue. The second five, the "do" qualities, specify what actions or attitudes should be undertaken, and for similar reasons. They are devotion, self-study, contentment, cleanliness, and austerity. These are not commandments but behaviors that reveal knowledge of Self and induce spiritual liberation when practiced properly, regardless of faith tradition. In that regard they are said to be universal, both in application and results, and hence have broad, enduring value.

DEVOTION

By total surrender to God, samadhi is attained.

—Patanjali, *Yoga Sutras*, 2:45

The one thing Spirit reputedly craves, yet will not demand, is our love. We can offer it genuinely and without coercion or, since we possess free will, withhold it. However, all souls innately seek God because they are individualized aspects of God; nothing short of union with the Divine can provide the complete sense of wholeness that all of us desire. Our yearnings, no matter how convoluted, can only be fully satisfied by God's love. Devotion is born of that truth and, seen in this light, is the path of love by which our souls return to their home in Love.

Devotion is vital for many reasons; it opens the heart, purifies the mind, and, most importantly, attracts grace. But loving Spirit for potential gain like receiving grace is inherently flawed. Devotion must be unconditional. Human relationships are similar. Nobody wants attention from those who do not genuinely care for them. On the other hand, the world becomes magical when we are alight with love: We would scale mountains or walk on burning coals for our beloved. That is devotion.

Everyone—including Spirit—wants this kind of love because it is selfless and pure. In fact, the Almighty reveals itself only when we seek it above all else. Accordingly, both devotion and technique are needed to scale spiritual heights. Train yourself to do everything for God as if you were doing it for your most cherished love. Not only does this attract grace, but it also has a wonderfully sweetening and uplifting effect upon the disposition. "If one offers Me [Lord Krishna] with love and devotion a leaf, a flower, fruit or water, I will accept it."[1]

Physical Application

People express devotion in many ways: lighting candles, burning incense, or being prayerful. Others chant or provide charity. Regardless of form, the important thing with devotion is intention. As just mentioned, Krishna commented that God accepts even paltry offerings if offered with right attitude. Likewise, Jesus praised the devotional generosity of an elderly woman who donated her last coin: "Verily . . . this poor widow hath cast more in, than all they which have cast into the treasury: For all they did cast in of their abundance; but she of her want did cast in all that she had."[2] So, it is not what we do but how we do it that makes actions devotional (or, in a familiar variant, what matters is not whether one wins or loses a game but how one plays it). Proper perspective applied to balanced action produces right behavior, which, when infused with devotion, becomes a potent force in attaining Self-realization.

Chanting is an especially potent practice because it brings energy (might) to the heart (love) and directs the attention completely (with all thy soul) on God. In my years of leading meditation groups, I have found that chanting effectively helps people get past their heads and into their hearts. Even persons with no spiritual leaning have reveled in the alluring aura generated by chanting. When practiced deeply, devotional chanting can induce a kind of intoxication similar to that which Jesus's disciples felt when touched by the Holy Spirit at Pentecost: Your energy gets elevated to a divine plane, and you simply get drunk on the love of God!

Another form of devotional practice involves using prayer beads or the rosary—whatever fits your tradition. The idea is to pass these beads between your fingers one at a time while reciting a mantra or prayer. Like anything else, it can either be an empty gesture or have inner value, depending on the quality of your attention and intention. One story tells of a woman who complained to a Hindu saint that prayer beads were ineffective: She had been using hers for years with no result. Discreetly observing her over time, he noticed that her attention was on everything else but God, so naturally her mechanical prayers would not bear fruit. The same can be said for any superficial spiritual practice. We could be in heaven but miss its glories if inattentive. With right determination and devotion, however, nothing can keep us from Spirit. Loving thought of God invites his company, and that can be done anywhere, anytime.

The love of God opens mental and emotional channels that keep us in tune with Spirit because Spirit is love. The Divine is omnipresent, and remembrance of God is a doorway to his presence. "Be thou diligent in performing actions in the thought of Me. Even by engaging in activities on My behalf thou shalt attain supreme divine success."[3] When thinking of and loving God, our vibrational field is raised. Ordinary persons may notice this rise by feeling joyfully inspired. Those steeped in divine ardor may experience spiritual ecstasy or, in the case of the Christian mystic Brother Lawrence, can levitate. When divinely enraptured, Brother Lawrence rose off the earth; his fellow monks, being ever practical, put him on refectory duty so the ceiling would keep him from floating away. Heaven, it seems, manifests wherever the head and heart are absorbed in God.

Why do some saints occasionally display unusual abilities when engrossed in Spirit? The primary reason is attunement. The limitations of natural law no longer apply after attaining oneness with the Divine. Those whose consciousness has merged into the unlimited have capacities to do extraordinary things because for them all is Spirit—including themselves. Masters who have attained such perfect divine unity describe the experience as awakening to their ever-inherent reality. It is not something one need acquire but, rather, must be realized directly. Once a wave resolves into the sea from which it arose, it grasps that it had always been part of the ocean and is, in fact, the ocean manifesting as itself. With awareness of our reality expanded beyond bodily confines to the infinite sphere of Spirit, we gain abilities that would otherwise be absent.

Such states are not intellectual but experiential, and those who are one with the Divine become channels for a power that has no limit in time, space, or expression. This attainment is the basis by which miracles can be performed; they result from operating laws that supersede those of nature.

Mental Application

Of the innumerable ways to cultivate devotion, I prefer two methods: practicing the presence of God and mental whispers. Of the former, the Bhagavad Gita comments: "He who perceives Me everywhere and beholds everything in Me never loses sight of Me, nor do I ever lose sight of him."[4] Practicing the presence is not complicated. It means trying to feel the presence of Spirit at all times and in every thing and person, everywhere, always. When done correctly, it creates a profound sense of closeness to God. A renowned Christian monk once demonstrated practicing the presence in a most unexpected way. Asked to say the invocation for a clerical gathering, he simply opened his mouth and spoke aloud the silent prayerful conversation he always had with God. For him, every moment was spent in the presence. To initiate your own process, start your day by saying "Good morning!" to God. Then invite Spirit to breakfast, to work, to the gym, out for dinner and a movie, whatever. As communion with the holy is made personal and intimate, devotion becomes easy. It is not strained like entertaining a stranger but sweet, like being with your dearest friend. The more you consciously and continually involve the Divine in everything, the more you will feel his silent, companionable presence.

Mental whispers is another way of drawing Spirit close through constant devotional calling. It involves using loving mental phrases or invocations such as "I love You," "Come to me," or "Reveal thyself." Metaphysically speaking, it is effective because whenever we want something enough, we think of it incessantly. Churning thoughts with continual longing creates a magnetism that draws the desired object. This magnetic force pulls Spirit to us and us to it when our God-yearnings outstrip material desire. Once I was stuck in an airport with hungover tourists returning from rowdy vacations. They were obnoxious, and I was becoming increasingly annoyed. Rather than descend into further distress, I chose to switch mental gears by silently calling to God. In due course I felt an internal energy shift that transformed my sour mood into one of patience, serenity, and inner sweetness. The situation had not changed, but I certainly had.

The trick is to do these practices constantly and daily, not just when there is dire need. With time, you note a significant change in how you relate to the world and how it relates to you. As we evolve spiritually, devotion becomes a natural reflection of our mindset. It infuses all we do and becomes the core of how we live rather than just another spiritual practice. Mother Teresa was a bastion of devotion. Bracketing her days with meditation and prayer, she constantly served Christ in the most wretched of humanity. By giving her all to God, whether through worship or service in the slums of India, she demonstrated a life that integrated devotion to Spirit on every level of activity. Hers was an outstanding example of how to live and be successful before God in this world.

Spiritual Application

Service to others is excellent because "others" are, in fact, us. Realizing we are all aspects of a common source helps reduce ego-consciousness and is a significant component of spiritual training. But transcending the ego through Self-realization is even better. Therefore, the highest manifestation of devotion is in the complete offering of our selves—body, mind, heart, and soul—to Spirit. This is achieved by meditation because through proper meditation our life force and consciousness are directed back to their source. All delusions of separateness melt away when we surrender fully. Devotionally purified, we may reclaim our divine birthright since God gives himself to those who give themselves to him. In truth, we are he. It is just the delusion of separateness that makes us think otherwise, and devotion washes that away.

This affirmation helps build an attitude of devotion:

> *I see, serve, and love God in all. Waking, sleeping, dreaming,*
> *thinking, working, playing, I give my all to God.*

SELF-STUDY

> *By study [of scriptures and the Self] comes communion*
> *with the Lord in the Form most admired.*

> —Patanjali, *Yoga Sutras,* 2:44[5]

Self-study is not narcissistic self-absorption, but the looking past physical appearances, waves of thought, and ripples of emotion to perceive the soul. One famous Indian saint, Sri Ramana Maharshi, was known for having devotees reflect deeply on a core question, "Who am I?" When presented with inquiries by visitors or disciples, he would often ask them, "Who is doing the asking?" Odd as this may sound, he sought to push them beyond the intellect to more divine depths. His training was comparable to that of Zen masters who used enigmatic koans like "What is the sound of one hand clapping?" to induce cognitive dissonance in monks and push them past mental limitations to direct intuitive realization.[6]

Self-study is meant to replace faulty self-perceptions with clear inner awareness; it propels us beyond the mirage of who we seem to be to the reality of who we truly are.

Physical Application

The modern spiritual teacher Ram Dass wrote about his crippling stroke in the book *Still Here: Embracing Aging, Changing, and Dying.* He examined aging and infirmity while drawing from his vast reservoir of insightful and compassionate self-study. In the book, scripted around personal challenges, he claimed that we all face potential frailty, confusion, and debilitating ailments. His point, and that of self-study, is to focus on our soul and not the body—which Saint Francis referred to as "Brother Ass."[7] The Self becomes a refuge when we are adept at this, and trauma may be experienced without attendant suffering. This point is important because pain of itself is not suffering. Suffering involves identification with discomfort as opposed to impartial recognition of its existence. Pain or pleasure may be unavoidable but need not define us when we are anchored in wisdom. We either learn endurance or, if able, retire to spheres of consciousness where agony has less dominion.

Here are a couple examples of exercising mental/spiritual detachment: Yogananda once used a painful accident to teach disciples what happens if the mind is kept on the spiritual plane. A concrete block fell on his foot, yet he remained unfazed. He then told them to watch as he brought his mind down into body awareness. Immediately his face broke into a grimace of pain. His purpose was to show how the cultivation of soul consciousness lets one inhabit a body yet not be dominated by the sensations with which we typically associate ourselves.

When another exalted saint, Sri Ramakrishna, lay dying of stomach cancer, a grief-stricken disciple asked how he could help. Groaning in pain, Ramakrishna reached out to clasp the disciple's hand. Oddly enough, the man began to feel increasingly joyful and eventually became intoxicated by bliss. Realizing what was happening he said, "Enough, Master, I see now!" The saint used this drama to reveal how his consciousness was not bound to the body or its ordeal. He inhabited a more sanctified sphere.

Such stories are not meant to minimize the body but to show how master souls may opt to handle painful circumstances.

In a certain light, self-study reminds us that life is purposeful yet fleeting. We are not meant to stay on earth forever; it is a temporary residence for education and refinement. Excess attention to the body and earth dramas cloaks a sacred evolutionary plan that impels us to recall who we are and rise above nature's dance of change. All creation—our bodies, this planet, the cosmos—is an enormous manifestation of that which alone endures: Spirit. When we unite with the Divine, we awaken from the dream spectacle of creation and become aware of being the eternal. This does not mean we lose our identity; rather, we realize that God has become us and we are, and always will be, one with him.

Mental Application

A fine example of self-study is revealed in how Herbert Benson and Jon Kabat-Zinn introduced meditation-like exercises and mindfulness meditation to the Western medical community. As a result, those inner technologies gained mainstream receptivity and have become not only acceptable but popular.

Herbert Benson, a Harvard cardiologist, was approached by Transcendental Meditation (TM) practitioners in the 1960s with a proposal that he study their brain and biological reactions to meditation. Initially resistant, he relented and was shocked to discover that meditation lowered blood pressure so effectively that persons afflicted with high blood pressure would be hard-pressed to find medications that worked as well. Benson was so intrigued by these results that he wrote *The Relaxation Response* and subsequently founded Harvard's Mind/Body Medical Institute. One of the first Western doctors to examine spirituality and healing, Benson has pursued related research ever since and has written and coauthored numerous scientific articles and eleven books bridging Eastern and Western medicine, spirituality, healing, and mind/body science.

Jon Kabat-Zinn, a behavioral psychologist, became a meditation icon in 1993 after Bill Moyers interviewed him for the television special *Healing and the Mind*. Kabat-Zinn was successfully integrating hatha yoga with traditional Buddhist mindfulness meditation for patients with chronic pain or high stress who had been unresponsive to traditional Western medical care. His outcomes were so beneficial that an applied program model was developed based on his work and chronicled in the books *Full Catastrophe Living* and *Wherever You Go, There You Are*. Given the efficacy of Benson's and Kabat-Zinn's efforts, the health profession—and the West in general—has far greater respect for meditation and body/mind training.

Of particular relevance to self-study is how Kabat-Zinn had patients watch their mental and life processes. Taught to observe thoughts, feeling, and reactions neutrally, his patients gradually began dissolving their identification with pain states. They saw that such experiences are not fixed conditions but streams of awareness linked by identifying with perception. Breakthroughs came as patients learned to refine their perspectives from being in constant pain to those that included pain-free periods. Freed from the onus of unrelenting misery, they could restructure their lives from chronic disability to viable activity. The potency of self-study allows one to perceive skillfully what is real and behave accordingly.

Spiritual Application

As mentioned above, Descartes' "I think, therefore I am," although an important notion, is nevertheless wrong. Consciousness does not arise from nothing, nor can it exist prior to existence. The correct expression is "I am, therefore I think," because the capacity to be must precede the ability to perceive. A spiritual life requires that we always seek the truth, for through it comes freedom. Self-study moves us past the ephemeral to the eternal. Realizing that we are projections of Spirit on the screen of duality brings emancipation from the duplicitous influence of cosmic delusion.

The following affirmation promotes the right attitude for self-study.

"I am not the body, nor the mind; I am Spirit, ever-new consciousness, existence, and bliss divine."

CONTENTMENT

By contentment, supreme joy is gained.

—Patanjali, *Yoga Sutras*, 2:42

Contentment is both an attitude to cultivate and the fruit of wisdom. It is a somewhat misunderstood quality that is occasionally misperceived as complacency. By yogic standards, however, it is considered the supreme virtue because it represents unflappable equanimity. In the world of relativity, control is illusory and success evanescent. Despite our best efforts, we can be healthy and wealthy one day, bedridden or impoverished the next. True contentment requires being anchored in divine states wherein the vicissitudes of life cannot shake one's core.

Physical Application

It is hard to give a physical example of contentment because it is not a thing you do. Rather, it is a mental quality nurtured by faith, understanding, and practiced composure. Life can be oppressive unless we look past the unreal to the real and accept the dualistic nature of this plane. Materiality prompts us to measure ourselves by its standards. Such assessments, however, only reinforce emotional reactivity to shifting circumstances. Legend has it that when the Buddha passed away, the chief of deities, Sakka, uttered the following: "Impermanent are all component things. They arise and cease, that is their nature: They come into being and pass away, Release from them is bliss supreme."[8] Only through right understanding and inner experience can reactive inclinations to outer events be replaced by enduring soul serenity. Being even-minded and cheerful in spite of life's inevitable ups and downs gives rise to contentment.

Mental/Emotional Application

Attitudes are principally matters of choice. When we stop waiting for things to go our way and consciously choose to engage life enthusiastically, regardless of circumstances, we assert our power to be happy. Flexing inner muscles of joy makes them strong, especially since deterrents to cheer seem to abound. Yet seldom do we recognize how much we can control our quality of life by right thinking and choosing not to get derailed by life's innumerable mishaps. Reality is objective, but our responses to it are subjective. Contentment is available to anyone willing to grasp it, especially when one is able to tap and hold on to positive states accessed in meditation. It takes practice, but if we insist on being joyful and vigilantly do not let negativity erode intent, we increasingly realize how attitude conforms to will.

Practical applications of contentment are innumerable. For teens, the desire for peer approval is paramount until they realize it means little. What matters is who we are, not what others think of us. This principle applies to people of all ages and for every kind of craving. As persons mature in wisdom, they realize that enduring satisfaction is only found within. With right effort, unhealthy tendencies toward fruitless pursuits become replaced by an equilibrium arising from being centered in the Self. Such states of contentment do not negate feeling or avoid life, but are mental havens that keep one serene amid the flux of life and duty.

Spiritual Application

Delusion induces stasis, confusion, restlessness, desire, and lassitude. It is aptly reflected in the famous song lyrics, "looking for love in all the wrong places."[9] Contentment counters these tendencies by replacing deleterious lures with the positive by-products of soul contact. In myriad ways, all of us strive for accomplishment, recognition, power, etc., until it dawns on us that what we truly crave is fulfillment, and that is a spiritual attribute solely accessed within. Quests for outer fame and fortune recede as innate soul qualities manifest more fully. Misguided outer pursuits are traded for the ever-abiding inner joy of Spirit, and we learn to live serenely without seeking gratification or definition from the world. We also stop fretting over past or future and let happiness manifest in the only time we have, now. After all, if our life quality were determined by random circumstance, we would always be at the mercy of mercurial happenstance. With the perfection of contentment comes freedom in the present moment and, ultimately, realization of a fundamental spiritual bliss that permeates all creation and beyond.

To promote contentment, use one of these affirmations:

Abiding within the Self, I accept all circumstances with joyful serenity.
I am happy now and always, complete within my Self!

In addition, try the following exercise:

With closed eyes, imagine everything meaningful in your life being taken away. Feel the sense of loss, even fear, as things disappear. Sit with that feeling. Explore the aloneness. Reflect on why the missing elements were so important. Did they make you feel loved, valued, approved of? Go deeper. Be present in the void, looking past emptiness. Let all feelings subside and ask yourself silently, "Who is the 'me' that feels?" and "What makes 'me' feel whole and happy?" Is it a person, an object? Note how these make you feel good, but not someone else. Realize that it is not the things or people that make you feel good, but your reaction to them. The feeling of enjoyment is not intrinsic to anything external, but comes from within you and is projected outwardly.

Now be still and feel joy directly. Imagine something or someone who elicits a sense of joy in you, then focus on that quality of joy itself, not what seemingly gave rise to it. Concentrate on that joy and sense it as an independent, preexisting aspect of yourself that is ever available once you know where to look and how to access it. Regardless of what life provides, takes, or denies, at your core you are independent, free, complete, and joy-full. Bask in this realization, feel it, and in that knowing, witness the birth of contentment.

CLEANLINESS

Moreover, one gains purity of sattva [existence], cheerfulness of mind, one-pointedness, mastery over the senses, and fitness for Self-realization.

—Patanjali, *Yoga Sutras*, 2:41

It may seem odd for cleanliness to be deemed a holy practice, but it is not about tidiness so much as purifying ourselves from anything that detracts us from Spirit. Spiritual yearnings and sacred insights increase naturally when the mind and heart become cleansed of material fixations.

Physical Application

From a strictly physical point of view, concentration on God is easier when we are not distracted by bodily conditions of filth, pain, or lust. The body is a temple in which Spirit abides as soul. When the mind is preoccupied with the temple, it cannot focus on the divine indweller. Imagine trying to meditate or pray with a pounding headache, itchiness, or cramp. It is extremely hard. The principle of cleanliness recognizes that a clean, healthy body frees the mind for spiritual pursuits, whereas one wracked by discomfort remains tied to contrary signals. Try bathing prior to your daily spiritual routine. Water eliminates surface debris, calms nerve endings, and purifies the energy field that surrounds the body. Just as cleaning a window allows in more light, auric cleansing removes subtle psychic "dust" that can impede refined perception. Also, before engaging in spiritual activity, it is beneficial to purify one's devotional setting. Methods for doing so include burning candles or incense, ringing gongs or bells, and, as some indigenous traditions do, smudging areas with certain herbs like sage, sweetgrass, or copal. Such practices create an uplifting atmosphere free of inharmonious vibrations.

Another aspect of cleanliness is dietary. The maxim "We are what we eat" has genuine merit. Athletes utilize training diets because of their impact on performance, and many faiths link preparation and consumption of food to more than nutrition. Some traditions maintain silence at meals to contemplate the divine imminence. Certain yogis will not eat in public or take food from persons deemed impure, claiming these factors convey disturbing vibrations. Like everything in the universe, food has subtle qualities, some of which uplift while others induce sloth or restlessness. The cellular intelligence in food conveys residual attributes on a refined level that affect mind/body states. This statement may seem extreme, but, again, it is not: Food has impact. Even Gandhi felt that governance of the palate helped bring the mind and sexual drive under control. On a gross level, poor diet generates excess waste that taxes the eliminative system. Efforts to remove wastes require energy that could be used in meditation. I appreciate and adhere to the advice of Yogananda's guru, Sri Yukteswar, who suggested that people find a simple diet that works for them and stick to it. If you eat flesh foods, try fish, fowl, or lamb over beef or pork, as the former have least negative impact. Periodic fasting (consult a physician if concerned about your health) is excellent to purge the body of toxins and to free the mind of certain habits. Cleanliness helps us on many levels, one of which is remembering that we are not the body and that, with training, we can live less by physical means (food) and more by the subtle energies that animate us. Aspects of this will be addressed later.

While purification is appropriate for spiritual training, it can draw misplaced enthusiasm. A woman who attended the same yoga-teacher training as I did venerated raw food. For her it was a necessity, and, like many zealots, she tended to reprimand anyone who did not share her views. My fondness for coffee was particularly egregious to her, so I savored the chance to share a message received in meditation: "Only love will make you pure." My attitude did not speak well of me at the time, but an old point of wisdom was made anew: "Not that which goeth into the mouth defileth a man; but that which cometh out of the mouth, this defileth a man."[10]

Paradoxically, the purpose for being embodied is to realize that we are not the body. To the degree cleanliness serves this end, dietary or otherwise, it is good. Beyond that, it can become an independent focal point that distracts us from the bigger picture. "Therefore I say unto you, Take no thought for your life, what ye shall eat, or what ye shall drink; nor yet for your body, what ye shall put on. Is not the life more than meat, and the body than raiment?"[11]

Mental/Emotional Application

Attitude is crucial. Consider how much time and energy is wasted on impure thoughts. Anger, lying, coveting, fear, lust, all reflect mental impurity. And to what end? We suffer. As with nonviolence, thought impacts feeling and impure thinking taints those who engage in such. Since thought creates according to type, we reap what we sow. When we are angry, we attract anger. When we are loving, we attract love. We tune in to universal frequencies that correspond to our own thoughts and subsequently bless or blast ourselves. Most importantly, impure thinking perpetuates delusion by reinforcing the lie of separation, whereas pure thought leads to salvation because it affirms unity and promotes harmony. Buddhism is especially astute in transmuting negative emotions.

One individual who models this training superbly is His Holiness, the Dalai Lama. Despite the Chinese government's longstanding repression of Tibet, the Dalai Lama has consistently advocated peaceful dialogue with them and not politically or spiritually unproductive responses of anger or violence. Tibet's situation is not yet resolved, but His Holiness's tolerance, compassion, and kindness have created more global support for the Tibetan cause than any call to arms ever would have. His nonviolent agenda is reminiscent of social battles waged by Mahatma Gandhi and Dr. Martin Luther King, Jr. Such spiritually pure action is not the way of the world, but it is ultimately most effective. One cannot help but be impressed by causes addressed through dialogue, principle, and prayer, not bloodshed. The subtle purity in such cases aligns with cosmic law such that if a cause is true and karmically just, the universe will inevitably support it.

Spiritual Application

Refinement implies quality achieved through eliminating impurities. When applied to people, the dross referred to is ego consciousness. Once that is removed, the presence of Spirit is self-revealed and gives a literal twist to the saying, "Blessed are the pure in heart for they shall see God."[12]

Impurity keeps the mind focused on the lowest strata of human interaction and, after a time, becomes tedious; there is just so much wantonness and base activity a person can engage in. Impurity leaves one feeling flat, like an uncarbonated cola. On the positive side, impurity reveals its own inadequacy: Pursuing the mirage of sensory happiness inevitably leads nowhere and provides an impetus to mend ways. On a deep level, we all want to behave righteously because doing so brings happiness. Sadly, ignorance and bad habits get in the way. To start walking on life's moral high road, eliminate impure thoughts and actions. Take baby steps toward more significant changes. Even when you falter or fall, do not quit. By depriving temptation of attention and energy, it gradually withers. Yogananda taught that the power of concentration resides between the eyebrows at the sixth chakra. To rid ourselves of bad habits, the brain grooves and subtle tendencies that support such patterns must be cauterized by directing the power of concentration from the sixth chakra to the brain. Doing so channels energetic currents that gradually "roast" the causative factors and elements that perpetuate wrong habits. In addition, by daily focusing on opposite positive qualities, affirming our innate purity, and perceiving the goodness in others, we gradually come to see the glory of God reflected everywhere.

The following affirmation helps create an attitude of purity:

> *The pure light of God shines within me, around me,*
> *everywhere. I am pure, for Spirit is within me.*

AUSTERITY

> *By austerity, impurities of body and senses are*
> *destroyed and occult powers gained."*
>
> — Patanjali, *Yoga Sutras* 2:43

Austerity is usually deemed an unappealing practice because it involves images of severity and deprivation. While abstaining from temptations and exercising righteousness can be difficult initially, it eventually proves rewarding. A companion to nonsensuality and self-control, austerity fortifies the will to reject alluring yet toxic sensory distractions. It destroys the stranglehold of bad habits and, most importantly, allows the soul to replace ego dominance with the rule of Spirit. In the Bhagavad Gita, the Spirit-led life is symbolized by Krishna (personification of God), who drives the chariot (the body) for the disciple Arjuna, (personification of the soul) as they battle the forces of evil (delusion) to restore righteousness (Self-realization) to the kingdom (consciousness). It is a metaphor for the epic battle all human beings must undertake to overcome ignorance and reclaim unity with the Divine. Through dour-seeming austerity or self-discipline, the greatest of victories is gained: clarity of conscience, inner emancipation, and bliss eternal. "To him that overcometh will I grant to sit with me in my throne, even as I also overcame, and am set down with my Father in his throne."[13]

Physical Application

To think anything in life can be achieved without effort is foolhardy. Accomplishments arise by transforming ideas into reality through methodically directing energy toward desired goals. Without such action, we remain ineffective dreamers. As Shakespeare's King Lear said, "Nothing will come of nothing."[14] One benefit of my martial arts background was discipline. I was actively training while most of my peers were actively partying. The latter is not atypical but can have dire consequences if not checked by prudent restraint. Life is not static, and people risk functioning on automatic pilot or slipping into decline unless they purposefully strive to advance. Austerity effectively means intentionality: It is the efficient application of energy to achieve desired outcomes and, in the case of spiritual pursuits, a significant cornerstone for attaining Self-realization.

From a classical yogic (spiritual practice) context, austerity refers to disciplines used to control the mind, body, and life force. Adepts who perfect such disciplines gain certain paranormal powers called *siddhis*.

The major (versus minor) siddhis enable those in possession of them to do the following:

- Become as small as desired

- Become as large as desired

- Make the body light by decreasing its specific gravity

- Make the body heavy by increasing its specific gravity

- Travel thousands of miles in the sky swiftly

- Stand on the earth yet touch the highest of things

- Attain desired objects

- Predict the future

- Attain clairvoyance, clairaudience, telepathy; read thoughts

- Understand all languages including those of animals

- Cure all diseases

- Stay underwater as long as desired

- Become invisible

- Spiritually enter the body of another

- Keep a youthful appearance as long as desired

- Control men, women, animals, and all elemental forces

- Restrain passions and emotions

- Become one with the Lord of the universe (those with this power can restore life)

Life force is the coin of our astral domain and must be enhanced, not depleted. As repeatedly stated, sensory abuse gives fleeting but dissipating pleasure, whereas conserving and raising energy to centers of higher perception in the brain yields lasting spiritual joy. In time, inner powers may also manifest as the soul sheds egocentric limitations. Such aptitude can seduce an unprepared mentality, causing a kind of spiritual materialism. Because of this, prudent adepts will not use their abilities unless inwardly guided to do so. The real value of austerity is not cultivating supernormal skills via arcane practices, but attaining profound realization through energy control. We need not focus on the fantastic so much as the essential: self-transformation. "He who overcomes others is strong; he who overcomes himself is mighty."[15] The capacity for immaculate self-control is miraculous enough. Once divine union is attained, use of any additionally acquired powers becomes relatively unimportant.

Two forms of austerity that almost everyone can safely practice are fasting and the exercise of moderation. Fasting purifies the body, calms the mind, deepens meditation, and helps free one from bodily dictates. Though uncomplicated and relatively easy to do, abstaining from food rends the fabric of familiarity and thrusts people past comfort zones. It can be daunting since we are conditioned to appease hunger, and many persons can't fathom not eating three square meals daily. Yet fasting is enjoyable once you get used to it. As a youth I envied athletes' ability to consume huge amounts of food. Now I find that large meals make me uncomfortable and dampen my spiritual sensitivity. As a rule, I fast once weekly and find that the respite from eating produces an enjoyable state of well-being. If you are intrigued by the idea, a simple fast involves just drinking orange juice and water as desired for twenty-four to thirty-six hours. If this is too challenging, switch to a mono-diet in which just one food, like apples or watermelon, is eaten for a similar time period. Keep fluid intake high while gradually lengthening the intervals between eating solid food. Eventually hunger becomes perceived less as cruel deprivation and more as a neutral sensation. The trade-off occurs when states of enhanced vitality, clarity, and calmness become evident. Experts have written volumes on fasting, so if you wish to fast do so under their guidance and check with your physician if you have any health concerns.

Fasting should never be used for weight loss, since it tends to lower the metabolism and is counterproductive to weight-reduction goals. Fast for purification or spiritual purposes only; pursue weight-loss agendas separately.

The second austerity, moderation, was dubbed the Middle Way by the Buddha. Described as a path between sensual indulgence and self-mortification, it is a teaching that, by necessity, must adapt to circumstances. Legend has it that the Buddha grasped the Middle Way while sitting near a river and hearing a lute player pass by in a boat. He realized that the lute's strings must be tuned neither too tightly nor too loosely to produce harmonious sounds, and subsequently pronounced it the correct path to tread for liberation. Despite this lovely anecdote, curbing inclinations is a challenge. We tend to ameliorate life's difficulties through comforting indulgences. Yet, rather than deprive ourselves of every reasonable pleasure, the key to moderation is mindful self-control, or doing the right things at the right time with proper attitude. Practice of moderation begins with vigilance. Vigilance is not code language for neurotic control but is the demonstration of will and intelligence exercised competently. Examine your routines to see where you can be more attentive. Sense when you have had enough food, drink, rest, exercise, and so forth. Notice when you lean toward excess, then engage restraint. Feel the equanimity of mastering inclinations. Gradually wisdom, not hedonism or habit, will prevail.

Mental/Emotional Application

The emotional application of austerity is not about frigid restraint, but about maintaining contentment by abstaining from unreasonable expectations. I often use relationship dynamics to portray this concept. When expecting fulfillment from others, we are often disappointed. It may not be wrong to want certain things, including a loving partner, but trouble beckons when we seek essential wholeness through another's affections.

This is a rapid route to romantic disaster. Hunger for love is natural and brings people together, but it most deeply reflects a spiritual yearning for divine union. Relationships are beneficial when they help us express love selflessly. Romance fails when people seek from partners the perfect completion that only God can provide. Austerity on this level helps us love and be loved without flawed assumptions. Though similar to nonattachment, in this context it reflects control of emotional energy surrounding expectation.

Here is a story to help illustrate this point. As a zealous youth new to hermitage life, Yogananda once asked his master if he could leave the ashram to seek God in the Himalayas. In response, Sri Yukteswar said, "Many hillmen live in the Himalayas, yet possess no God-perception. . . . Wisdom is better sought from a man of realization than from an inert mountain." Yogananda went anyway, but various ill-fated incidents revealed the error of his ways, so he shamefacedly returned to the ashram. Upon his arrival, Sri Yukteswar greeted him warmly and began preparing food. Surprised by such kindness, Yogananda asked why he was not rebuked instead. Sri Yukteswar replied, "Wrath springs only from thwarted desires. I do not expect anything from others, so their actions cannot be in opposition to wishes of mine. I would not use you for my own ends; I am happy only in your own true happiness."[16]

Through this incident Yogananda discovered the real meaning and demonstration of unconditional love. Austerity when rightly exercised frees energy from misguided traps and allows it to be applied in the highest manner. In the case of emotions, it produces an inner freedom that gives rise to personal serenity and a clement spirit.

Spiritual Application

My father used to comment succinctly, "One must give in order to get." Austerity in spiritual matters is the exercise of select disciplines to achieve divine ends. Not a function of grand or painful displays like lying on a bed of nails, austerity in its highest form entails the sacrifice of ego, the restraint of energies that nourish the false self to cultivate realization of the eternal Self. Yet even here it is necessary to avoid extremes in such pursuits and remain mindful of their purpose. Too often, the means to promote inner awareness become ends and replace the notable reasons for which they were originally undertaken. In the West, this condition is especially true in yogic circles where "doing yoga" is mostly about body-centric hatha exercises, not the real purpose of yoga—uniting soul to Spirit—which hatha is meant to serve, not replace. This remonstration applies to all similar missteps. For instance, a friend mentioned a workshop she heard of that was supposed to integrate mantra practice with tantra. She chuckled because those were code words for spiritually flavored sex training, alternately dubbed "chant and pant." Clearly something is not right when venerable disciplines are co-opted for ignominious purposes. Lest I digress overly, austerity is not an end unto itself but a rung on the ladder of self-development that elevates whoever uses it rightly to attain illumination.

The five austerities listed below are gentle, yet yield significant benefit if done properly. Although they may seem challenging for total beginners, I encourage trying them anyway, yet incrementally. Practice whatever feels attractive for as long as you are comfortable with it, and in time you should find them genuinely rewarding. Baby steps can lead to big accomplishments.

- Fast on orange juice once weekly and fast once a month for three consecutive days.

- Exercise moderation in all things: exercise, diet, sleep, work, socializing, etc.

- Maintain silence one day per week. When resuming speech, speak mindfully.

- Meditate twice daily; periodically meditate three to six hours at a time.

- Abstain from gossip and negative thoughts or feelings.

This affirmation is useful for reinforcing a mindset of austerity:

By will and wisdom, I control my self to liberate the Self.

The code examined in the past two chapters is a comprehensive tool for spiritual development. It shows us how to live in the world yet not be of it. By adhering to these ten precepts in thought and deed, we foster realization of and live according to the tenet of divine unity. Because they are so important, it behooves us to conclude our review with an integrated overview. The prohibitive elements are nonviolence, nonlying, nonstealing, nonsensuality, and nongreed/nonattachment. While there are many layers to these injunctions, one succinct interpretation shows how nonviolence produces harmony, nonlying manifests truth, nonstealing reveals cosmic law, nonsensuality uncovers soul joy, and nongreed invokes freedom. The five prescriptive elements are cleanliness, austerity, contentment, devotion to spirit, and self-study. Cleanliness purifies the mind and heart, austerity fosters self-control, contentment produces equanimity, devotion attracts grace, and self-study facilitates realization. Each quality corresponds with others in a complex play of interrelationship: cleanliness to nonsensuality, contentment to nongreed, austerity to nonstealing, self-study to nonlying, and nonviolence to devotion. Of course, they all relate in more comprehensive ways to form an essential integrative system of self-management that brings out the best in any who practice them. Most significantly, these precepts fashion a lifestyle of Spirit. Each is a tool for refinement and inner awakening. Apply them, and watch the positive changes that happen to and through you. Your efforts—in thought, word, and deed—are important, because as we become brighter, others are lifted from darkness as well. By the power of one, many are lifted.

We create our destinies. When mind is properly guided, we hasten to God; when misdirected, we sink deeper into delusion. So, free your Self. Learn to behave! Cleanse the consciousness through righteousness and attain the kingdom within.

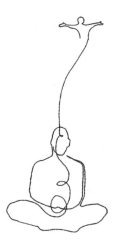

8

Energy: Building and Focusing the Life Force

A huge element for success in any spiritual endeavor involves building and focusing energy. And though not everyone shares my childhood relish of comic books, most people enjoy heroes or the qualities they represent. I have long suspected that imagination is a psychic forerunner of tangible reality and that mythic materials, from Homer's *Odyssey* to Superman, have a secret source in unconscious archetypes. Mixing the holy with the fantastic may seem unlikely, but we often project externally, through tales and legends, what we possess internally. Heroes are fashioned by quests and trials; comic titans often appear after spectacular transformations. In real life, saints are forged by devotional perseverance amid extraordinary circumstances. Epic battles of light and dark played on the stage of fantasy reflect the spiritual contest between good and evil within us. Where comic heroes use superpowers to combat wrongdoers, sanctified souls draw on Self-realization to defeat delusion. In fact, divine champions in the guise of illumined masters are periodically, and intentionally, sent into the world during times of spiritual darkness to manifest the light and redeem others:

> Whenever virtue declines and vice predominates, I incarnate on earth. Taking visible form, I come to destroy evil and re-establish virtue.[1]

For God sent not his Son into the world to condemn the world, but
that the world through him might be saved.[2]

Ingredients of heroic power, real or imaginary, are energy, will, and
intention. Energy is force, will marshals that force, and intention directs
it, for better or worse. Hitler demonstrated the dark side of energy
whereas Jesus, Buddha, and Krishna reflected only the light. Lacking
abundant energy, we usually pass through life without significant impact;
with it, we can shape destiny.

Energy, known as life force, alternately called chi, qi, or prana, must be
fostered and channeled to be beneficial. To do so necessitates proper cultivation, removal of blockages, and correct use.

Cultivating Energy

This process requires an integrated understanding of what the source of
energy is, then how to harness and apply it effectively.

As repeatedly stated, creation is inseparable from its Creator. The
creative act begins as thought emanating from Spirit, is condensed to
omnipresent energy—the subtle force that forms and animates all
creation—and concretizes into increasingly dense vibratory expressions
that eventually manifest as the causal, astral, and physical realms. In
short, the source of energy is Spirit.

Physical exercise is routinely touted as a key ingredient to "feeling
great," yet, while necessary for general health, it does not add life force.
That occurs solely by drawing upon the nimbus of cosmic energy that
surrounds and infuses each human being. None of us could live without
it. To illustrate, just as toy planes, cars, and boats may be remotely operated by radio waves, humans are similarly powered by universal life currents. This energy is dispensed automatically in amounts relative for each
person but can be augmented to boost mind/body functions and, most
importantly, enhance inner growth. Ways to increase this "allowance" are

often found in select yogic and tai chi practices that specialize in life force control and development. When asked which of the two systems to recommend for such purposes, I defer. Both have merit and should be chosen according to innate preference. It is prudent to learn details about each method and evaluate their teachers or students to see if they demonstrate the benefits of practice. I personally use an exercise series from my tradition to enliven the body/mind. The principles of these Energization Exercises, developed by Paramahansa Yogananda in 1916, are sound, and the routine is both healthful and invigorating. I will share more about these below but first need to point out that energy-building practices, regardless of type, should be used in conjunction with meditation to enhance inner realization.

The key to such practices generally lies in the use of will, breath, movement, or, as in Yogananda's method, conscious physical tensing. Willpower is critical because it summons life force surrounding the body, and specific patterns of breath, movement, or tension infuse it into us. To grasp this process more fully requires a brief reference to the chakras, since they are our internal energy centers. The term *chakra* stems from the Sanskrit *cakra* and was earliest referenced in the Vedic Upanishads. Being intrinsic to human mind/body/soul functioning, they are present in the esoteric teachings of all major religions: Buddhism, Judaism, Taoism, Islam, and even the mystical branches of Christianity.

Chakra means "wheel" or "circle" and refers to hubs of energy that animate and sustain the body and mind. They are aligned in an ascending column from the base of the subtle astral spine to the top of the head, and each has a distinct color and sound, and physiological, mental/emotional, and spiritual impact. Chakras also have two energetic poles, one negative and the other positive. The sixth chakra is central to energy dynamics because it is the principal center through which life force enters and is directed throughout the body. Its negative pole is situated near the base of the skull at the medulla oblongata, while its positive pole is the spiritual-eye center located between and slightly above the eyebrows.

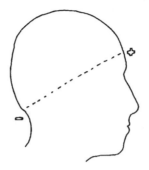

Among other things, the sixth chakra is a locus of will and the gate that allows additional energy into the body through proper attitude, intention, and application of right technique. The Energization Exercises utilize a process that combines focused will and conscious tension/relaxation to infuse energy into specific body parts. Simple as this seems, the theory is not. The process involves directing vital forces that perpetually surround the body into select areas by will-induced muscular engagement. This muscular engagement activates a process that channels life currents to the brain via the medulla oblongata, routes them through the subtle circulatory system—*nadis* or meridians—and transmits them into the physical nervous system and relevant body tissues as directed. Other methods of energy cultivation may achieve similar ends differently, yet the underlying principles for doing so are usually uniform.

Before proceeding, let me share an experience I once had with the Energization Exercises after a transatlantic flight. As is often the case in such trips, sleep gets badly compromised. On this occasion, my wife and I arrived in Amsterdam with sufficient layover time to visit a museum before catching our next flight. Unfortunately, jet lag was making me dizzy, and the idea of sightseeing was neither appealing nor very feasible. Under the circumstances, the best option for salvaging our excursion involved finding a discreet spot for me to do my recharging exercises. Fortunately, I did, and with immediate positive effect. Vitality coursed back into my system, eliminating all but trace elements of fatigue with no residual dizziness. I could resume touring with appropriate enthusiasm.

Though the practical body/mind benefit of these exercises was indisputable, I must be a stickler to my own rules and comment that energy-cultivation practices are primarily meant to enhance meditation and inner growth. Keeping a correct perspective on these matters is necessary to avoid the kinds of tangential involvements discussed earlier.

Eliminating Energy Obstructions

Consider the body as a complex bioenergetic machine. Though not a romantic perspective, it is a true one. As with any mechanism, whatever obstructs or depletes the fuel compromises its function. Since bodies fundamentally run on life energy, blockages of this force impair performance. Conditions causing impediments include spinal misalignment, nerve impingement, bad diet, injury, and negative or inharmonious attitudes. To achieve Self-realization, the body should be managed well but without fussiness or attachment. Using proper fuel like food and life force, keeping waste elimination effective, maintaining organ and limb health, and promoting efficient electrical conduction through the nerves and meridians are all critical for optimal psychophysiological-spiritual functioning.

Food

While not a high priority for everyone, appropriate diet makes a qualitative difference in mood and performance. Just ask elite coaches if they care what their team members eat. An optimal diet for spiritual "performance" consists of foods that have an elevating or high vibrational influence and do not clog the system, i.e., fruits, vegetables, nuts, whole grains, and dairy if your body can tolerate it. Red meat, refined flours, sugars, inappropriate fats, starches, and processed items should be minimized if not eliminated. Eat what is nourishing and not simply what tastes good. Add supplements if your nutrition is poor. Supplements might be advisable for everyone anyway since many foods come from nutrient-depleted sources, but do not become imbalanced. Choose a manageable, healthy diet that works for you and stick to it. For more information on these matters, I recommend *Eating Well for Optimum Health: The Essential Guide to Food, Diet, and Nutrition* by Andrew Weil. His authoritative and inclusive approach makes him a valuable, balanced resource.

Elimination

Few things feel as uncomfortable as constipation. Fortunately, proper diet that includes plenty of water promotes healthy elimination. If you are sluggish in this area, consult your healthcare provider. However the issue is addressed—diet, exercise, or spinal adjustment—the goal is regular removal of toxins from the body. Here are some basic tips to help keep your system operating well.

Fasting

Fasting one day per week and for three consecutive days once per month is usually quite safe. Orange juice is excellent for removing many impurities, including those from excess meat intake. Grape juice can help induce elimination. Fibrous bulking agents like psyllium husks, oat bran, or flaxseed can be mixed with water or juice to enhance the eliminative process, as can a natural laxative. The latter, however, should be used only during a fasting period. Cease laxative use once fasting ends unless medically necessary and prescribed.

Breathing

Proper breathing is vital for physical health, mental calmness, and spiritual practice. Not only does it oxygenate the blood, but it also removes metabolic waste, boosts body/mind function, and promotes life force intake and circulation, plus it sharpens meditative focus. The energetic elements associated with breath are highly regarded and advocated in yogic disciplines.

This is a safe, gentle breathing exercise to begin with:

- Exhale slowly through the nose while mentally counting from one to six.

- With lungs empty, hold the breath and count from one to six.

- Inhale slowly through the nose, counting from one to six.

- Hold the breath, counting from one to six.

- This concludes one cycle.

- Repeat this cycle eleven times.

This exercise series can be done three times daily. Longer breathing rhythms such as eight-eight-eight or ten-ten-ten may be used, but it is prudent not to exceed a twelve-twelve-twelve count. Be sure the breath proportions remain consistent throughout the regimen.

Bathing

Most people feel better after a good soak or shower. Especially when using a loofah brush, bathing is excellent for removing topical dirt, excess dead skin cells, and toxins secreted through the pores. The electromagnetic aura is purified by water, plus adding mineral salts to a bath can be therapeutic as well as relaxing. For such a simple act, bathing provides great collective value.

Nervous System/Circuitry

Perhaps the most crucial area of energy obstructions abides in the physical and subtle nervous systems. As mentioned earlier, meridians, or nadis, carry life force to the sensory-motor nerves, which in turn conduct electrical current throughout the body. Both are vital for proper systemic functioning. Seek treatment from appropriate healthcare providers like physical therapists, neurologists, osteopaths, or chiropractors if physical nerves are injured or their current is impinged by spinal misalignment. An acupuncturist or skilled energy healer may be consulted if the subtle life force is blocked or congested. The goal for every nervous system or energy-related treatment is balanced life force circulation and full restoration of nerve transmission. When that is accomplished, a feeling of overall physical and mental wellbeing inevitably prevails.

CORRECT USE OF ENERGY

There is no dramatic secret to maintaining physical health. Fundamentals include proper diet, elimination, exercise, and rest. Since the body/mind relationship is very real, a positive mental attitude should be included, too. Having briefly addressed diet and elimination, let's look at exercise, rest, and attitude.

Exercise

Engage in moderate, sweat-inducing aerobic activity three to six days per week for twenty to sixty minutes per session. Take no more than two days off between sessions. If able, add resistance activities like weights or calisthenics along with flexibility training. Resistance exercises offset decreased bone density and loss of muscle tone that come with age or hormonal changes. Stretching maintains range of motion, helps reduce stress, and promotes ease of movement. Exercise must be ongoing to be effective, so design a sustainable program that fits your timetable and is enjoyable.

Rest

Adequate sleep is crucial for the nervous system and overall body functions. Experts advocate different sleep quantities according to various age groups, but quality of rest is more important than time logged in. While many adults require eight hours of sleep per night, if one feels fully refreshed after only six hours, or even four, that may be sufficient. The body's innate intelligence will promote balance if not interfered with by excess caffeine or other stimulants. And speaking of balance, do not rule out naps; they have increasingly recognized restorative and performance-enhancing capabilities. Heed what the body requires to operate in a vital and enthusiastic manner.

Attitude

Research has proven a corollary between attitude and immune-system responses. Negative attitudes make us more susceptible to the common cold and flu. Anger and fear trigger the release of chemicals into the blood-stream that can become harmful if sustained over time and in such cases have been linked to various acute or chronic diseases. On the opposite spectrum, positive mental states are tied to longevity, improved stress response, and cardiovascular health. As Saint Paul wrote, "Finally, brethren, whatsoever things are true, whatsoever things are honest, whatsoever things are just, whatsoever things are pure, whatsoever things are lovely, whatsoever things are of good report; if there be any virtue, and if there be any praise, think on these things."[3] And you will likely have better health to boot.

Avoiding Energy Depletion

Abundant energy enriches personal, professional, and spiritual potential. Depleted energy is equally influential, but in an opposite manner. Therefore, whatever drains our vital resources must be vigilantly avoided. The three most energy-robbing culprits are overindulgence in food, sex, and negativity.

Food

The nutritive aspects of food were briefly discussed earlier. Here we discuss food specific to energy depletion. Abuse of food, both in kind and quantity, stresses the digestive system, causing the body to shut down. Compare eating a vegetable salad at lunch versus a plate of lasagna; the latter will likely induce significant drowsiness by midafternoon. It is not that pasta is bad, but heavier foods require more energy to process than lighter fare. The rule to follow is eat to live, don't live to eat. Keep meal portions modest and select foods appropriate for your needs in alignment with the dietary guidelines provided earlier. Avoid eating too much or, for that matter, too quickly. The stomach takes almost twenty minutes to register being full, so push back from the table when feeling comfortably satisfied. Exercising restraint with food is challenging because food often serves to reward or comfort. However, the payoff of a slimmer waist and greater vitality is worth it.

Sex

Sex nowadays is looked at much like a sport. Participants are judged by skill, frequency, and aptitude. If it were an Olympic event, it would undoubtedly attract the most athletes. From a biological perspective, sex is strictly a reproductive act. That is a view many people choose to ignore or use to keep kids out of trouble for as long as possible. On an emotional level, sex may be a means to share intimacy or express romantic feelings. All too often it is simply a primal drive for which people crave fulfillment. Men in particular seem endlessly creative in finding ways to indulge. And frequently! Sex uses tremendous amounts of life force, and, with the exception of sexual addiction, modern trends lean toward unfettered indulgence: The more the merrier, if that is your preference. Constraint is not even on the menu of behavioral options. From a metaphysical perspective, sexual activity drains vitality and can have a deleterious effect on the nervous system if pursued excessively. Spiritual adepts encourage self-control, moderation, or celibacy to promote mind/body health and spiritual development. Advocates of celibacy claim that abstinence enhances a potpourri of beneficial by-products: inner realization, mental peace, memory, fortitude, willpower, cognition, digestion, vitality, and equanimity. Control of sexual energy is also said to facilitate supersensory perceptions that are more gratifying than mundane ones.

Obviously this topic is a minefield, since people inevitably find ways to rationalize whatever they wish to do. That does not negate the subtle impact associated with expending energy sexually. Since the sex drive is so imperious, second only to self-preservation, suppression can lead to psychological or social problems. Therefore, persons serious about their spiritual efforts are counseled toward moderation. Sublimation of sexual energies must be done gradually and willingly to wean off the primal compulsion. This energy can be transmuted with right attitude, under-standing, and technique. Directing it into alternate channels can yield such highly refined states of perception that engagement in sexuality at those times becomes undesirable. I can personally attest to this experi-ence and have found that sublimation can be attractive, not depriving. Yet, as with everything related to spiritual growth, an appropriate time arrives when this sort of pursuit may be explored. Until then, it is best to practice moderation and not force an agenda one is not ready for.

Negativity

Medical science has established a definite relationship between attitude and health. Negativity compromises bodily functions, whereas positive thinking can enhance them. This linkage is also correct spiritually. Enthusiasm stimulates willpower, which facilitates increased life force intake. Upbeat individuals often abound with energy, while the reverse is true for persons with inharmonious attitudes. Negativity decreases the distribution of vital force, causing fatigue, agitation, and debilitating moodiness. Consider how we tire when confronted with undesirable chores, yet when a lover calls we come alive, even if we were previously exhausted. The reason for the change is attitude. Willingness opens energy gates; unwillingness closes them. I once found myself begrudgingly taking out household trash. I adjusted my attitude and gained energy after realizing I would gladly help a friend with this duty. The point is this: Say Yes! to life—all of it. Smiling when you do not feel like it can seem hypocritical but can nevertheless have a remarkably uplifting effect on mood. This perspective was shared by Piotr Winkielman, professor of psychology at the University of California, San Diego, when he remarked, "The human mind is much more attuned to facial expressions—including ones barely noticed—than people might realize. Our mind becomes very practiced at picking up cues, whether it's smiling or frowning. Smiles can activate a process in your brain that basically makes you more positively predisposed to whatever comes next."[4] So the next time you begin

130

slipping into a funk, command yourself out of it. It is not always easy. Life can be a battle for joy. But practice the art of being happy—right now and for no reason. It is a habit that, once learned, continues to pay immense dividends. The proverb "Smile and the world smiles with you, cry and you cry alone" is often quite correct. Attitude makes a huge difference in life.

Energy Basics

Building and focusing life force can be tricky, so it is worthwhile to review the basics. For starters, here is a warning: Energy exercises can be extremely potent and, if not practiced correctly, can severely damage the nervous systems. Students have hurt themselves from rash activity, so I strongly advise receiving instruction from expert teachers, not just books. Texts impart information in a generalized way, whereas instructors can assess student weaknesses and vulnerabilities to tailor regimens accordingly. In this book I only use safe energy exercises that anyone can do. The following overview presents fundamental principles of the practices I will cover in the next chapter.

Modern science recognizes that matter and energy are interrelated, separated solely by rates of vibration. Ancient yogis realized that even these hail from the subtler substance of divine consciousness. Accordingly, every human is made up of three increasingly dense and interpenetrating bodies: one of thought, another of energy, and the third, the densest, of matter. This complex unit is surrounded by a nimbus of life force that enters and animates the body via an astral portal at the medulla oblongata. That energy is apportioned automatically, but willpower coupled with correct technique can increase the amount of vital force taken in.

Tension is usually associated with muscular or psychological stress but in our context refers to how energy manifests when it floods the body. Consider muscle flexing. As mentioned earlier, this set of actions draws life force into and through the nerves, thereby triggering processes that result in muscular contraction. The same may be said of all sensory-motor experiences. Vital energy transmitted via nerve wires facilitates physiologic responses. Our body machinery cannot operate without energy moving through the nervous system.

Relaxation depicts an opposite state where energy withdraws from the body. In the muscles, this registers as limpness; in the sense organs, it registers as an absence of function. In both cases willpower—either consciously or unconsciously applied—is central to the infusion and withdrawal of life force. Paralytics, for instance, may want to raise their arms but cannot due to nerve damage; the will is engaged but not the means to access energy. On the other hand, hale individuals may be able to use their arm, but refuse to do so. Here the energy is available but not the will. In both situations, will is required for life force to flow, yet energy must be accessible to be applied effectively.

The sensory nerves conduct energy automatically, whereas its movement in the motor nerves is mostly voluntary and, again, prompted by will. Select body areas become charged with vital force when muscular contractions are practiced intentionally and correctly. Reversing this process induces relaxation by withdrawing energy from the body. We want the capacity to both infuse and retract energy at will.

Try this experiment: Make a gentle fist with your right hand and squeeze it lightly, gradually increasing the intensity until the right forearm vibrates. Notice how your will directs energy with progressive vigor until the fist and forearm tense accordingly. Now reverse the process. Will the energy to recede and the area will become limp and heavy.

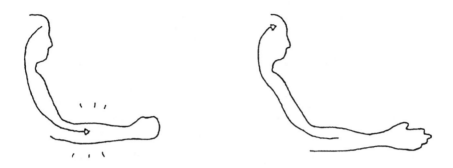

When this method is applied to any body part it, will charge and then relax the area, creating an effect of vitalized calm. With practice, this process increases awareness and control over energy, a definite asset in spiritual training. Learning to relax and withdraw energy from the body is a precursor to directing it to higher centers of spiritual perception, and that is what meditation practice is all about.

9

Chakras, Life Force, and Breath: Energy Exercises

I n this chapter, we move more deeply into the application of practices that have a direct impact on consciousness. Principles addressed in a broad manner previously are now given more concrete expression through specific energy exercises that enhance spiritual awakening when done regularly and with right attitude. Dedicated repetition of these activities is necessary, for it creates subtle mental pathways that effectively balance, clarify, and heighten our awareness.

PREPARATORY ENERGY-INFUSING EXERCISES

These first three exercises reduce fatigue and stress plus prepare one for meditation. Practiced singly or collectively, seated, lying down, or standing, they share a common operating principle: "The greater the exertion of the will, the greater the flow of life energy into a particular body part."[1] In laypersons' terms, this principle reiterates what was shown in the fist-tensing experiment in the last chapter: A correlation exists between the amount of will a person uses and the degree of energy mustered. Just as an electrical dimmer switch regulates current flowing into and back from a light bulb, thus affecting its luminosity, tensing the body—or parts of it—from low to high levels incrementally draws in more vital current until the body bulb shines brightly. In performing these exercises, the core of each muscle group should be gradually infused with energy *that results in physical tension*; then that energy must be gradually and fully withdrawn, causing a subsequent state of relaxation. Doing so charges the atomic structure of all impacted cells and then facilitates a state of calm repose. It is important to practice attentively with correct imagery and a willing attitude.

As a general rule, do these energy-infusing exercises in fresh air, and, whenever possible, open a window or go outside to harness the augmenting power of sunlight. Visualize solar radiation pouring into the medulla oblongata or spiritual eye. This vibrant energy is absorbed through the skin and, in proper amounts, helps the body manufacture vitamin D, plus it provides energetic nutrition to the cells. A certain amount of sunlight is excellent for health despite valid ozone concerns. Doing these exercises in direct light should not pose a health risk because they can be done relatively quickly, but consult your doctor if concerned. Never rush the exercises or move too rapidly from one to another. Haste compromises the process and its purpose. Savor the sensations each provides, and bask in the fruit of your efforts after every session. As previously mentioned, sensitivity toward energy is preparatory to controlling it, and the more adept we become at controlling it, the more we can direct energy by concentration and will alone.

The full series of Energization Exercises is available through Self-Realization Fellowship or other organizations that share Yogananda's teachings. I teach them through personal instruction. (To learn about this and related services I provide, see www.Awake-In-Life.com.)

Preparatory Focus

- Run your fingers down the back of the head until a soft spot is felt at the base of the skull. This is where the medulla oblongata is located.

- Picture a halo of cosmic energy surrounding you, with small streams of life current steadily pouring into the body at the medulla oblongata.

- With eyes closed or half open, direct your inner gaze to the spiritual-eye center, the seat of divine will and concentration located between and slightly above the eyebrows.

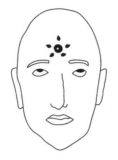

- Gazing into the spiritual eye, visualize the medulla center openly receptive to increased life force entering the body.

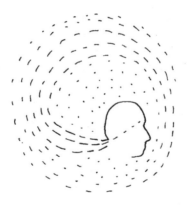

Part 1: Total Body Exercise

- Inhale through the nose in a double breath, a short breath followed by a long breath. (It sounds like hih, hihhhh.)

- Hold the breath and gradually infuse the entire body with low to high levels of energy by tensing it incrementally until it vibrates. Hold this high-level tension for several seconds.

- Exhale through the mouth using a double breath, a short exhale followed by a long one. (It sounds like huh, huhhhh.)

- As you exhale, simultaneously relax completely.

- Repeat three to twelve times.

- Notice the aftereffect of increased aliveness coupled with a sense of calm ease.

Part 2: Individual Body Part Exercise

Proceed as follows using the same principles described above:

- Focus at the spiritual eye, yet drop your awareness to the left foot.

- Concentrate on the center of the left foot.

- Tense that area from a low to high level until the entire foot vibrates with energy.

- Visualize light emanating from that center point and bathing the foot in life force.

- Now relax and feel energy withdraw from the foot. Imagine it retreating up into the spine and going to the spiritual eye. Take your time to feel the impact.

- Repeat the procedure with the right foot.

- Slowly and mindfully apply this process to the following body parts in correct sequence:

- Left calf, then right calf

- Left thigh, right thigh

- Left hip and buttock, right hip and buttock

- Abdomen region below the navel, then abdomen region above the navel

- Left fist and forearm, then right

- Left upper arm, then right

- Left pectoral region, then right

- Left lower back, then right

- Left midback, then right

- Left upper back and shoulder, then right

- Left side of neck and throat, then right

- Front of throat and neck, then back side of neck

- Double-inhale, tensing the entire body together from low to high.

- Hold the tension briefly, then double-exhale and relax fully.

- Concentrate on the sensations of soothing vitality.

Do this entire sequence once, or twice if so desired.

Part 3: Tensing Upward-in-a-Wave Exercise

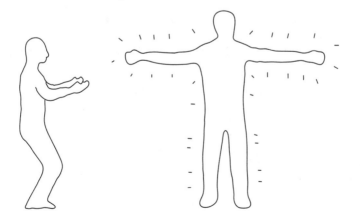

- Stand with feet shoulder-width apart for balance.

- Stretch the arms out to the sides at shoulder height, hands open and palms facing forward.

- Double-exhale through the mouth (short, then long) and bend the knees slightly while bringing the outstretched arms forward in an arc to the front of the body as if clapping. Relax briefly, completely, and feel.

- Double-inhale (short, then long) through the nose, straighten the legs, and pull the arms/fists apart in a gradual arc to their original, shoulder-high outstretched position. Simultaneously tense the body upward in a wavelike sequence, beginning with the feet and ascending to the head.

- Hold this position for two to three seconds while tensing fully.

- Open the hands, double-exhale, and repeat the initial relaxation step (third step in this sequence).

- Repeat this sequence three to twelve times, being attuned to your body/mind responses.

Rub and Renew Exercise

This easy, invigorating technique is wonderful for stimulating blood and energy circulation. Though excellent prior to bathing, it can be done anytime to perk up when feeling sluggish or as a finishing exercise after completing a hatha yoga session.

The palms contain minor chakras that serve as portals through which life current flows. This flow is also the basis of "laying-on-of-hands" healing.

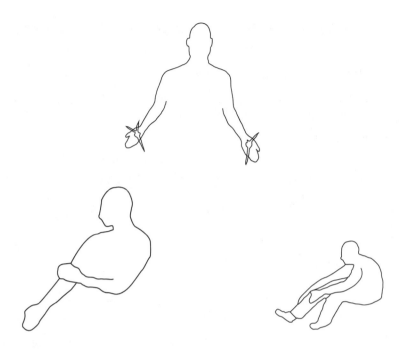

- Rub the hands briskly until they become hot. This stimulates the healing force in the palms.

- Next, move the right palm briskly up and down the left arm for five to ten seconds.

- Now switch and use the left palm in a similar fashion on the right arm.

- Use both palms to rub the left and right thighs simultaneously, then, rub the abdomen.

- Make fists and gently but vigorously rub the lower back on both sides.

- Gently tap the skull with the knuckles. This is good for the brain and memory.

- Rub both hands together again and put the heated palms over your face and eyes. Visualize (and feel) that you are absorbing the energetic warmth.

- Finish by gently lowering your hands and gradually opening the eyes.

Do this sequence on bare skin, or over your clothing if the former way is not feasible. Enjoy the pleasing sense of stimulation, and combine this sequence with other energy exercises to give yourself an added boost.

Stretching

Stretching is such a potent exercise that it demands special attention. Just as athletes know the relevance of stretching to performance, yogis recognized the value of stretching as a subtle warm-up for meditation. As ice must melt to assume a watery form that satisfies thirst, energy has to be freed from bodily constraints to be used as spiritual fuel. Stretching does just that; it melts "frozen" energy that has been stuck in the body as muscular tension. People often cannot begin calming their minds until their bodies have been addressed. For this reason, I spend ample time incorporating stretching into my introductory meditation programs: It is *that* helpful. Especially in the early stages of developing a spiritual practice, stretching helps relax the mind, thereby creating a fertile inner environment in which the seeds of meditation can take root.

Stretching has many spiritual values, including:

- Energy is the link between mind and body.

- Energy infused in the muscles produces movement or tension.

- Energy stuck in the body causes chronic tension.

- Physical tension can cause mental tension and vice versa.

- Gentle stretching releases stored muscular energy.

- Energy circulating freely promotes physical ease and mental harmony.

- A relaxed body and calm mind are needed to perceive subtle spiritual realities.

Almost everyone can benefit from gentle stretching regardless of age or flexibility, though it is advised to consult a physician if you are pregnant, have had recent surgery, or have other health concerns.

The key to stretching is to tailor efforts to your individual ability and body type. The goal is not extreme flexibility but the release of trapped energy. Regular practice and a relaxed attitude are the main ingredients for success.

Stretching is most effective when it is done after a few energy exercises and just prior to meditation. This helps maximize life force cultivation, circulation, and utilization. Stretching prior to meditation can take as little as five to ten minutes. You can do less, or more, but many individuals are strapped for time and need to economize their efforts. Positive results will accrue from consistent practice of manageable amounts. And remember, some stretching is better than doing none at all.

How to Stretch

As with anything, there are right and wrong ways to stretch. Bodies are designed to protect against injury, so proper stretching must be done correctly, that is, in a relaxed, sustained fashion. Practice calmly and mindfully while you are imagining the joints, muscles, and spine moving smoothly, as if lubricated in oil. Think of loosening the body versus pushing it; the former invites a relaxed mental framework, whereas the latter induces a sense of tension. Your practice should feel pleasing, like the gentle, full-body morning stretch that many do naturally upon awakening.

Never extend yourself to the point of pain, hold your breath, or bounce. Bouncing is an antiquated approach that looks beneficial but actually contracts muscle fibers instead of releasing them. Monitor the body for strain and, if detected, stop, then restart in a more relaxed fashion. Remember, you are striving to enhance inner peace, not win a gymnastic event through grueling effort.

A correct three-step approach is:

1. Go to the point of feeling mild resistance. Hold for ten to thirty seconds.

2. As the muscles slowly release, hold for another ten to thirty seconds.

3. Relax and feel. Enjoy the various sensations that arise during practice.

Stretch Model

Phase One	Phase Two	Don't Do!
Easy Does It	*Go Deeper*	*Drastic Stretch*
(Hold for 10–30 seconds)	(Hold for 10–30 seconds)	(Avoid!!!)

Some general breathing guidelines while stretching are:

• The breath should be slow, balanced, rhythmic, controlled.

• Exhale when bending forward or sideways.

• Inhale when returning to center or upright positions.

• Never hold the breath. Breathe constantly and smoothly.

• If breathing is labored, you are not relaxed. Ease up and breathe gently.

To recap, keep mentally relaxed; this will allow the body to stretch more easily. The goal is to release energy for use in spiritual practice. Honor body rhythms, which change daily. Do what feels good and right.

Stretch Series

The following series of seated stretches can be used by anyone, including those with physical challenges, in lieu of a hatha yoga manual. Standing or supine stretches may be added to the routine if you wish. The series is easy, effective, and modeled after programs I have developed for corporate wellness programs. Those interested in learning more about stretching will benefit greatly from the classic book *Stretching* by Bob Anderson.

This seated routine starts at the head and works down, using gentle rotations and elongation movements.

1. Neck Rotations

Sit in a comfortable, upright posture. Lift the shoulders to protect the backward arc of the neck. Then, keeping the shoulders elevated, drop the chin forward and gently roll the head around in a smooth, easy circle. Repeat three to six times in one direction, and then switch directions.

2. Neck Extension/Flexion/Turns

Inhale and gently lift the chin, tilting the head back as far as comfortable. If concerned about your neck, raise the shoulders to protect against over-extending backward. Exhale and lower the chin to the chest, extending the back of the neck. Repeat two to three times.

Inhale and return the neck to center, or what I call neutral position. Exhale and turn the head to the right as far as able. Inhale and return to center. Exhale and turn the head left as far as able; pause, inhale, and return to center. Repeat several times.

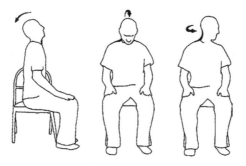

Neck stretches stimulate the fifth chakra, which is a center of divine peace located in the throat region.

3. Shoulder Rotations

Roll the shoulders forward several times in large circles; then reverse directions and roll them backward, also in large circles. (Option: Placing the hands on top of the shoulders in a winglike fashion helps to isolate the area.)

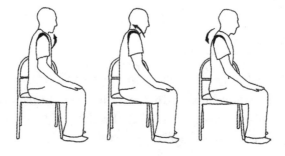

4. Shoulder Lift and Squeeze

Inhale and raise the shoulders toward the ears. Hold and tense in that position briefly. Exhale, drop the shoulders, then relax. Repeat several times.

5. Shoulder Release and Chest Opener

Clasp the hands behind the back. Straighten the arms, roll the shoulders backward, and gently raise the arms/joined hands as high as possible. Feel the shoulders and front of the chest stretch. Hold ten to fifteen seconds, then release. Repeat as desired. (This stretch helps stimulate the fourth chakra, in the heart.)

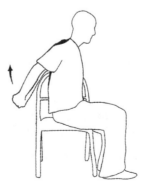

6. Joined Arm Stretches

Inhale and raise the hands overhead. Link the fingers together, then turn the palms face up. Exhale, elongate and straighten the arms, pushing the palms toward the sky. Inhale and feel the sides and ribs stretch upward. Hold the position (not the breath!) for fifteen to thirty seconds. Keep breathing gently throughout the process, and notice how each breath adds to the stretch.

During exhalation, lower the arms in front of the body with fingers still linked and palms pressing forward to stretch the arms and middle/upper back. Hold for fifteen to thirty seconds, keep breathing, then release the hands, drop the arms, and feel the aftereffect sensation.

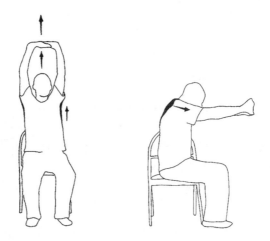

7. Isolated Arm Stretches

Raise the right arm, bend the elbow, and stretch down behind the head as if trying to scratch your midback. Bring the left hand to the right elbow to deepen the stretch. Hold fifteen to thirty seconds; switch sides.

Stretch your right arm across the chest. Grab it at the elbow with your left hand and gently pull the right elbow toward the left shoulder. Hold fifteen to thirty seconds. Repeat on the opposite side.

8. Side Stretch

Raise both arms overhead, hooking the thumbs together with palms facing forward, as in a diver position. Stretch the arms to the right as far as comfortable, hold fifteen to thirty seconds, then return to center. Repeat to the left side. (These stretches promote feelings of tranquility.)

9. Forward Spinal Stretch

Spread the feet about eighteen inches apart. Put the hands on the thighs or knees, whichever is more comfortable. Exhale and slowly bend forward from the hips, keeping the spine long and relaxed. Let the head/neck/trunk hang down as far as possible without straining. Rest the palms on the floor and hold for fifteen to thirty seconds. Return hands to knees or thighs. Inhale and, using the hands for support, lift the head/neck/trunk back to center. (Forward bends help open the spine for energy to flow more freely.)

10. Backward Spinal Stretch

Slide to the front of your chair. Cup the palms to the small of the back; straighten, and lift the spine and neck; raise the chin gently; roll the shoulders back, then bend backward as far as comfortable. Keep breathing and hold for fifteen to thirty seconds. Return to center by coming back in reverse order: Release the backward stretch of the spine, relax the shoulders, and relax the palms. Repeat several times as desired.

Here is an alternate approach: Slide to the front of the chair. Raise arms overhead, keeping them straight with palms pressed together as in a prayer position. Next, stretch the arms backward as far as comfortable in a gentle arc. Breathe and hold, then return to center by reversing the process. (Backward bends help push energy down the spine.)

11. Spinal Rotation

Inhale and lengthen the spine as if pushing the crown of the head upward. Keep both feet flat on the floor, put the left palm on the right thigh, and twist slightly, reaching behind you with the right hand to grasp the chair or wherever is comfortable. Exhale and gently turn the neck to the right, then rotate the entire torso similarly. Push lightly into the turn with the left palm, and pull slightly with the right hand. Hold fifteen to thirty seconds, breathing fully. Release the twist, inhale, and return to center. Switch hand positions to the opposite side, exhale, and twist to the left accordingly. Repeat both sides one to three times as desired. (These stretches help squeeze energy through the spine.)

12. Hip Opener

Sit upright and place the right ankle on top of the left knee. Holding the ankle steady with the left hand, use the right hand to gently press the right knee down toward the floor. Hold fifteen to thirty seconds, then switch sides. Repeat as desired. (Hip stretches boost comfort in seated meditation postures.)

13. Leg Stretch

Sit forward in your chair with left foot flat on the ground and right leg straightened in front. Lightly thrust the right heel forward and pull the right toes back, causing the right foot to flex. Inhale, sit straight, and then exhale and bend forward as far as possible, without straining, over the right leg. Use your hands for support on the right leg, and stretch the torso/head toward the foot. Hold this position for fifteen to thirty seconds. Inhale and return to upright position, using the hands to assist you. Switch and repeat on the left side. Repeat the entire exercise as desired. (Leg stretches help eliminate a sense of restlessness.)

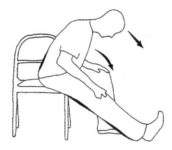

14. Thigh Stretch

Move to the front and right side of your chair—just make sure you don't fall off! Grab the left side of the chair with your left hand to remain stable, and then lift the right knee upward until you can grasp the right ankle with your right hand. Hold the ankle, drop the right knee toward the floor, and pull the right ankle/heel to the buttock. Hold this position for fifteen to thirty seconds, remembering to breathe. Now place the right foot on the floor, slide to the left side of the chair, and repeat the stretch on the left side. Repeat the entire exercise as desired. (Thigh stretches induce feelings of calmness and poise.)

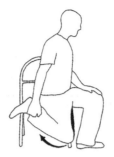

This concludes the basic stretch series. Actual practice time should not exceed more than five to ten minutes once you are familiar with them. Longer sessions, or those that include additional stretches, may be done if desired. Remember, these are warm-ups for meditation and not a focus unto themselves.

Some may think stretching or energy exercises are irrelevant within the framework of their religion. I maintain that diverse faiths can, and perhaps should, incorporate practices from other traditions if doing so enriches spiritual insight. For instance, some Benedictine monks and nuns incorporate tai chi into their spiritual regimen because they feel it brings them closer to God. Similarly, I use yogic sciences to promote spiritual growth as I understand it, but I am not Hindu. The essence of spirituality is not to get bogged down by doctrines or rituals, but to grasp and apply universal principles so they can beneficially impact your direct experience of Spirit regardless of faith orientation.

CHAKRAS

Everyone, regardless of ideology, shares an energetic anatomy governed by subtle principles. When inner growth is undertaken in an esoteric and scientific fashion, not through traditional external rituals, learning to control the vital energy currents is a definite asset. Learning this skill is enhanced by familiarity with the chakras. Some attention to the sixth chakra was provided earlier when discussing the will in relation to energy movement, but now we broaden our scope and add valuable information about the other chakras.

Western medical science sees our organic process as a complex interplay of physical tissues, chemicals, nerves, bones, organs, and synaptic activity. Yogic science maintains that an energetic or astral body is integrated within the physical body and provides the vital substructure for the latter to function. Chakras are part of that astral anatomy. They are hubs of life current that receive cosmic life force after it enters the body via the medulla oblongata and flows to the brain. That force is then routed through subtle channels into the chakras, which correspond with the cerebrospinal nerve plexuses and direct energy into the physical nervous system. In short, chakras are distribution centers for vital currents that govern body/mind operations. But they are more than that; they have a very special role in our level of consciousness and inner growth.

Chakras manifest archetypal aspects of the cosmic creative process. These aspects, referred to as earth, water, fire, air, ether, and superether, are not physical elements but energetic principles. Each has certain constituent characteristics or qualities that infuse all creation, including us. As such, chakras not only fuel the operation of our bodies, but influence our mental and spiritual states as well. This process will become clearer as we progress.

The Seven Chakras

CHAPTER 9

In the human body there are seven primary chakras. Much has been written about them, so here is a very basic overview:

1. The *Muladhara* chakra is called the earth center and is located at the base of the subtle spine, by the coccyx. It governs primal physical and emotional functions of elimination and survival and mental traits of tenacity, plus it facilitates compliance with the first five spiritual attributes of the Code of Illumination: nonviolence, nonlying, nonstealing, nonsensuality, and nongreed.

2. The *Svadishthana* chakra, or water center, by the genital area governs reproduction and mental/emotional flexibility and spiritually enables adherence to the second set of five code attributes: devotion, self-study, contentment, cleanliness, and austerity.

3. The *Manipura* chakra, or fire center, sits near the navel region and impacts physical digestion, mental creativity, personal power, and spiritual self-control.

4. The *Anahata* chakra, or air center, sits midchest near the heart and directs cardiopulmonary activities plus emotional feeling. It is a nexus between the lower chakras, which primarily govern physical functions and awareness, and the higher chakras, which address our spiritual composition and powers. Energy here stimulates love, which can either be raised up to Spirit and transmuted into perfect, unconditional, divine love or directed outwardly in ordinary human ways that are marred by personal likes, dislikes, and desire. The heart is a crucial center in spiritual evolution and the focus of much attention in all spiritual traditions.

5. The *Vishuddha* chakra, or ether center, is nestled at the throat. It impacts oral communication and the capacity to assert truth, plus it is the seat of spiritual calm.

6. The *Ajna* chakra, or superether center, also known as the spiritual eye, is slightly above and between the eyebrows. It affects frontal lobe function

and the power of concentration and will, and is the gateway to Christ consciousness or union with God throughout creation. When seen correctly in meditation, it is a deep blue circle surrounded by a halo of gold in the very center of which sits a five-pointed white star.

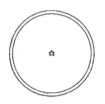

7. The *Sahasrara* chakra, or crown center, at the top of the head represents the domain of pure Spirit. When our consciousness is fully immersed in this center, we experience union with Spirit in and beyond creation. Souls fixed in the cosmic consciousness associated with this center attain permanent liberation, or complete freedom from delusion and compulsory rebirth.

Familiarity with the chakras usually stems from Eastern influences, but the universality of their impact has been depicted by mystical experiences from saints of all traditions. The following anecdote is an example of such as recorded by Saint Theresa of Avila in her book *The Interior Castle*:

> As I write this, by the way, I can't help but wonder what's going on inside my own head. Those noises I told you about in the beginning are getting so loud that it's almost impossible for me to obey the order to write this. It sounds like there are a multitude of rushing rivers inside my head, their waters cascading downward, surrounded by many little birds and other whistling sounds [sounds of the chakras, to be explained later]. This is all unfolding not in the ears but the upper part of the head, where they say the higher part of the soul

resides [sixth and crown chakras]. I have spent long periods in these regions. The spirit seems to push its way upward with great power and speed [kundalini rising]. . . . All of this turmoil does not hinder my prayer or interfere with what I am trying to say. Instead, my soul is whole within its quietude, its love, its longing, and its clarity of consciousness.[2]

This is a fine description of inner energy manifestations experienced during states of elevated spiritual experience.

ENERGY PATHWAYS

We know that vital energy flows through the body in channels called nadis or meridians. Two primary channels, called *ida* and *pingala* in yogic vernacular, border and intersect the spine at nerve junctions where the cerebrospinal plexuses are situated. These "power lines" carry most of the current necessary for healthy body/mind functioning. Between them, in what is called the central astral spine, lies a third vital conduit called the *sushumna*. It is the pathway by which the dormant spiritual force known as kundalini can be raised to fully activate the chakras and induce divine illumination. Dubbed the "serpent force" because it lies coiled at the base of the spine and ascends in a winding serpentine fashion, kundalini has no other literal or metaphysical connection to snakes and certainly is not satanic. Yogic sciences have historically called the ascension of this force "kundalini awakenings." The various ecstasies of Saint Theresa of Avila reflect this experience, as does the biblical reference to Moses having "lifted up the serpent in the wilderness."[3] In this case, *serpent* refers to kundalini energy and the *wilderness* implies withdrawal from the world in meditation.

A visual representation of this energy schematic (the ida, pingala, sushumna and kundalini) is depicted in the caduceus, the staff of Hermes and the modern symbol of the medical profession.

In Greek mythology, Hermes was a master healer, among other things. His staff later became the symbol for Hermeticism, a broad yet esoteric movement that operated across centuries and whose roots stemmed from ancient Greek, Egyptian, and other traditions. In brief, the staff depicts twin ascending snakes, which correspond with the principal life-current pathways, ida and pingala, while the central pole around which they intertwine is the deeper energy conduit, the sushumna. The wings at the top symbolize the spiritual freedom achieved when these currents ascend and unite at the crown chakra.

In addition to distributing life force throughout the body, chakras are rungs on the "Jacob's ladder" of higher consciousness. Specifically, in ordinary waking states, energy circulates through the ida and pingala, during which time the consciousness remains fixed in the material realm. Certain practices can be used to withdraw energy from the physical senses, and two main astral channels then direct it into the central sushumna canal and up the chakras. During this ascension, the chakras are said to open completely, causing superfine perceptions of the soul and other subtle spiritual realities. Once these forces crest at the crown chakra, the soul's consciousness, heretofore identified with the body, merges into Spirit. Maintaining such high states of consciousness over time dissolves all spiritual impurities, past karma, and deluded identification with the body and bestows final and complete reunification with Spirit. This process is the esoteric basis for the biblical passage, "To him that overcometh will I grant to sit with me in my throne, even as I also overcame, and am set down with my Father in his throne."[4]

The yogic sciences understood that spiritual growth is ponderous and ordinarily requires much time to attain complete evolution and freedom of the body/mind/soul. By mapping the descent of energy and consciousness into the body, plus identifying their movements, manifestation, and impact, they developed specific techniques that could raise these forces back to their source. Meditation and energy control are critical to this spiritual effort. They are the scientific, nondenominational, and universally viable means to expedite reunion with the Absolute.

LIFE FORCE AND BREATH

Many esoteric traditions link breath with life. While breath is not life, it is intimately connected with the movement and control of life force. Practices like kundalini yoga or the Kriya yoga method of Paramahansa Yogananda are but two systems that harness special breath-related methods to raise life force up the central astral spine, sushumna, to facilitate the awakened spiritual states described above. Those techniques are too advanced to share here. Instead, I share more suitable exercises that balance vital forces and serve as a first step toward mastering them. Adhere to these guidelines for optimal results. If, or when, more advanced training is desired, seek qualified personal instruction.

Breathing Exercises

A principal feature with breathing exercises is that mental states respond to the depth, rhythm, and retention of breath. Regulated breathing balances energy movement through the brain hemispheres, causing a tonic effect that enhances nervous and immune system functions. Associated benefits include resistance to stress and disease, plus elevated mood, calmness, focus, and creativity. Even a little done daily is beneficial.

Exercise 1: Centering Breath

This exercise is a cornerstone for stress management and can be done anywhere, anytime—at home, driving (with eyes open!), or at work. It helps us be present and turn within for meditation when desired. In fact, many spiritual traditions use centered breathing in conjunction with prayer or guided imagery to enhance inner experiences.

- Sit in a comfortable position with body relaxed and spine straight. You may also lie down if circumstances allow, but it is often easier to remain awake and alert when sitting upright.

- Close the eyes and mentally focus on the breath.

- Clasp the hands together, placing them gently on the stomach.

- Inhale deeply and slowly through the nose. Let the belly expand. Imagine drawing an elixir of calmness directly into the body and brain.

- Exhale slowly and fully through the nose. Allow the belly to release. With each exhalation, let go of all mental worries and physical tension. Experience a sense of increasing physical heaviness. Retreat within and drop awareness of the body. Enjoy being interiorized inside the bodily shell.

- Repeat the inhalation and exhalation process smoothly and continuously.

- If the mind wanders, return it to observing the breath.

- Do not try too hard or judge yourself. This is not a contest.

- Practice five to ten minutes.

- When finished, inhale fully and gently return to "normal."

When done repeatedly, the positive effects will make you want to do more.

Exercise 2: Full Yogic/Diaphragmatic Breath

All breathing in this exercise is done through the nose. This exercise is most easily learned while lying down but may also be done seated or standing. As the basis for many breathing exercises, it should be practiced regularly until proficiency is attained.

Phase One: Lower Abdominal Breath (like the Centering Breath)

- Lie on your back with closed eyes, and focus on the breath.

- With thumbs on the navel, palms on the stomach, and fingers relaxed, inhale low and deep to inflate the lower abdomen. Exhale fully, and let the stomach settle back. Relax.

- Repeat three times.

Phase Two: Rib-Cage Breath

- Glide the hands up to the outer sides of the ribs.

- Inflate the abdomen as in phase one, but continue inhaling until the breath expands the ribs laterally.

- Exhale in reverse order: Release the rib cage first while maintaining a still-inflated belly; then release the belly. This controlled isolation takes practice. It might help to keep the stomach lightly pushed out during the rib release, after which the belly can be contracted to force air out. Relax momentarily before repeating.

- Repeat three times.

Phase Three: Upper Chest Breath

- Keep one hand on the side of the rib cage and another on the chest/sternum.

- Inhale and sequentially fill the belly, ribs, and upper chest.

- Exhale in reverse order—from upper chest, ribs, then belly. Relax.

- Repeat three times.

This kind of body/breath isolation also takes some practice but can be mastered readily.

Phase Four: Complete Diaphragmatic Breath

With hands down at your sides, palms face up, or with one hand on the belly and another on the chest:

- Do the entire full-breath sequence (belly, ribs, upper chest) in a smooth, unforced flow.

- Exhale in correct reverse order and relax.

- Repeat three times; then be still and disregard all breath.

- Surrender now. Float in serenity until you wish to resume normal activities. Then inhale gently several times, roll onto your side, and rise gracefully.

Exercise 3: Breath of Light

This technique integrates a standing version of the full diaphragmatic breath along with palm-chakra imagery. Called "Breath of Light," it manipulates energy while you visualize it as a force of healing light.

Before proceeding, practice this experiential exercise: Rub the hands until they are hot. Separate them by several feet, then slowly bring them toward each other. Feel for sensations in the palms. If you are not aware of any, repeat the process with closed eyes to enhance subtle perception. See if you can discern: 1) an invisible cushion between the palms, as if they are pushing against an intangible resistance, or 2) rapid acceleration when the palms draw near, as if an attractive force is compelling them together.

What is happening? If magnets are placed end to end, they either attract or repel, according to polarity. Magnetism is a by-product of energy, and, as our bodies are bioenergetic, vigorous rubbing intensifies energy fields and corresponding electromagnetic responses. Creating energetically charged hands makes it easier to feel our life force and the magnetic charge in the palm chakras. The Breath of Light uses energy coursing through these minor chakras to cleanse our magnetic field by sweeping the palms over the aura with healing intent.

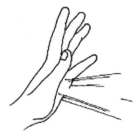

Life force emissions can balance or cleanse the energy field plus strengthen or recharge it when we visualize energy pouring into the aura. When done properly, a sense of vitalized purity is experienced.

Try the exercise now. All breathing should be done through the nose in a gentle, continuous manner.

Part One: The Inhalation Phase

- Stand in a relaxed posture, hands hanging loosely by your side.

- Exhale and bend forward as far as comfortable, keeping the knees relaxed and not locked.

- Rub the palms together vigorously, as in the warm-up exercise.

- Turn the palms so they face the front of the body.

- Inhale slowly and begin standing upright, keeping the palms directed in toward you.

- Visualize energy pouring out from the palms and bathing your body in light.

- Imagine inhaling positive qualities like joy, peace, or vitality.

- Continue this inhalation and visualization until the palms are at head height.

- Raise the hands overhead, extending the palms up to the sky in a gesture of receptivity. Here, you should be at the fullest point of inhalation.

- Hold the breath briefly.

- Envision healing light pouring down from the heavens into the palms and into you.

Part Two: The Exhalation Phase

- Exhale slowly, lowering the hands in front of the face, palms again pointing inward.

- Visualize light shining out from the palms, bathing you in a cleansing, enlivening radiance.

- Continue lowering the light-emitting palms over the upper body and torso.

- Bend forward, knees relaxed, no straining, while shining light over the lower body—thighs, legs, and feet.

- Let all negativity—fatigue, illness, and worry—be washed away.

- When bent over fully, pause to flick the fingers as if getting rid of energetic "goop" gathered during the cleansing exhale.

- Now start over. Inhale, stand slowly, and again visualize the palms infusing light and positive qualities into the body/mind. Stop when the hands are fully overhead in the receptive position.

- This completes one full cycle. It is perfectly safe to do six to twelve full cycles.

- To finish, with hands overhead, exhale and visualize surrounding the body in a sphere of light by lowering the palms, face upward, in a descending arc that terminates at your sides. Feel the peaceful aftereffect. Hold onto that peace as long as possible.

The Breath of Light exercise is excellent for removing negative energies acquired during the day from upsetting people or environments. It is also beneficial for ridding oneself of foul moods, fatigue, and psychic distress.

Exercise 4: Balancing Breath

Breathing practices affect the brain. Certain breaths stimulate the left-brain hemisphere, enhancing analytical, logical, and linear abilities. Others affect the right hemisphere with its intuitive, artistic skills. The next two exercises balance both brain hemispheres equally.

Part One: Simple Balancing Breath

- Inhale through the nose for a count of ten.

- Hold the breath for a count of ten.

- Exhale through the nose for a count of ten.

- This makes one cycle. Do six cycles.

A variation of this exercise enhances lung capacity and oxygenation by increasing the breath count with each cycle. For example, cycle one may be done for a count of eight, cycle two for ten, and so on until the last cycle is at, or near, twenty. The inhalation, hold, and exhalation pattern of equal count should apply to all cycles.

Part Two: Alternate Nostril Breath

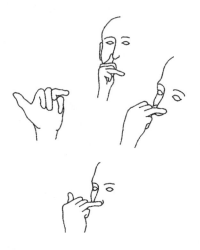

- Close the right nostril with your right thumb.

- Inhale through the left nostril for a count of eight.

- Keep the right nostril closed while also closing the left nostril with the third finger—next to the pinky—of the right hand. If you have trouble coordinating that finger, use any finger on the right hand.

- With both nostrils kept closed, hold the breath for eight.

- Now release the thumb from the right nostril and exhale through it for a count of eight.

- Immediately afterward, inhale through the open right nostril for an eight count.

- Close both nostrils as before and hold the breath for eight.

- Release the right third finger and exhale through the left nostril for eight.

- This makes one complete cycle.

- Begin again, but try increasing the breath by two counts with each new cycle—eight, ten, twelve, fourteen, sixteen, eighteen, etc. Start with three cycles and work up to six.

Again, if you cannot coordinate the fingers exactly as described, do what works easily for you.

Now that you have a selection of breathing exercises to choose from, the question arises of which to do, when, and why. Experiment with each for a week or two in the order given. Go slowly; become familiar with each, and let the nervous system adjust to their impact. Then, create a routine or combination that works for you under different circumstances. For instance, I use the Centering Breath whenever a calming stress-management tool is needed. The Full Diaphragmatic Breath and Breath of Light are great with hatha yoga practice or after being in unsavory environments. I do Balancing Breaths or Alternate Nostril Breathing prior to meditation. But this is my pattern, not something everyone must do. The idea is to use the exercises to balance energy and thereby enhance focus, clarity, meditation, and related activities. As with any system, proficiency is developed with practice. Do not be impatient. These are subtle activities that manifest results gradually but assuredly if done with patient persistence over time.

ENERGY REVIEW

Let's briefly review key principles about energy and its corollary, magnetism. People are souls, sparks of the Infinite Spirit encased in three external bodies: causal, astral, and physical. These bodies function because energy and consciousness form, fill, and animate them. Everyone receives an allotment of vital force that can be increased by proper diet, exercise, attitude, absorption of sunlight, and tapping cosmic energy.

CHAPTER 9

According to natural law, wherever energy exists, so does magnetism, and the greater the energetic flow, the stronger the magnetic field. Electricity produces magnetic effects, and magnetism produces electrical effects. The relationship between the two, called electromagnetism, is one of the four fundamental forces in the universe. The elements discussed here are not quasi-scientific theories divorced from the common laws of physics, but more subtle or metaphysical aspects with spiritual relevance and lifestyle application. While energy is relatively one-dimensional, magnetism is not. How we apply energetic forces creates magnetic qualities that affect the kind of person we become. As light flowing through colored glass takes on its tint, when we expend energy in certain ways, our consciousness and magnetism assume attributes of these activities. For instance, if individuals invest energy in cultivating their sexual allure, they will develop a corresponding sexual magnetism. Such carnal appeal is popular in a worldly sense but is of a lower moral and vibrational range. What we want to develop is spiritual magnetism, the kind cultivated by higher-vibration, divinely focused activities. To accomplish this, it helps to learn about more subtle magnetic principles and how to apply them.

Magnetic Vibratory Exchange

Magnetism flows from stronger sources to weaker ones. It passes between people's hands, feet, head, eyes, and thoughts, even by gazing at or listening to others. With so much energy being exchanged unconsciously, it is tremendously important to choose one's company and environment wisely. Just by concentrating on another person, your mind becomes tuned to his or her vibrational frequency—like a television or radio station—and subsequently draws both positive and negative traits from that person. That is how sensitive the nature of mind and energy is. Therefore, it is prudent to avoid associating with, thinking about, or discussing degrading people. Concentrate instead on the uplifting actions, thoughts, and insights of spiritual individuals; tap into their influence, and your own growth will improve. Since we must interact with a range of people every day, focus on their positive characteristics instead of their lesser ones. Doing so energetically stimulates commendable attributes in both them and you.

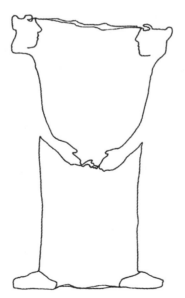

Here are some excellent tips for developing positive magnetism:

- Keep physically fit.

- Eat a pure diet with plenty of fruits.

- Maintain strong, erect posture.

- Move with deliberate vitality.

- Avoid sluggish behavior or moodiness.

- Strive to be positive and enthusiastic.

- Focus 100 percent on one thing at a time, yet be able to shift attention as needed.

- Listen more than talk.

- Combine sincere feeling with intelligence.

These practices enhance the amount and quality of your energy because they open the door to cosmic vitality and draw on its unlimited abundance. If skeptical about such claims, try the following experiment—but only briefly: Slouch, become self-absorbed, lazy, dour, and eat junk food. Remember, this is meant to be a trial, not a lasting change! Notice how unattractive you feel and how others regard you less favorably. Then switch behaviors. Become sincere, focused, attentive, and vibrant. Even if you do not feel this way initially, assume the consciousness until your pretense becomes reality. As your mindset and energy shift in positive ways, you will experience increased physical and mental well-being plus find that others are attracted to you. Positivity is self-rewarding and benefits everyone because we are all connected.

On Spiritual Magnetism

Energy must be directed in sacred ways when we wish to develop spiritual magnetism. On a mental level this involves being kind, loving, compassionate, joyful, harmonious, truthful, humble, devotional, and wise. On a physical level it entails fasting, prayer, service, meditation, and related disciplines.

Spiritual realities are not part of a distant heavenly domain; they coexist with us wherever we are. By expressing them through right thought, right word, and right deed we take on their qualities and transform ourselves. In addition to having an elevated lifestyle, one significant factor to promote inner awakening is attunement with vessels of the Divine—saints, saviors, or scripture. This attunement is an important yet subtle aspect of spiritual practice: "But as many as received him, to them gave he power to become the sons of God, even to them that believe on his name."[5] Although this phrase was deconstructed earlier, it alludes to spiritual attunement according to the laws of energetic affinity and magnetic exchange created by concentrated thought on illumined souls. As Swami Sri Yukteswar stated, "To keep company with the Guru is not only to be in his physical presence (as this is sometimes impossible), but mainly means to keep him in our hearts and to be one with him in principle and to attune ourselves with him."[6] Focusing on such exalted souls tunes the mind to their attributes, energy, and consciousness, thereby raising one's vibrational field to higher, sanctified levels. When striving for such attunement, visualize the eyes of a chosen saint and gaze receptively into them. Try feeling divine consciousness pouring from them into you. Remember, cultivating true receptivity is not passive. "But be ye doers of the word, and not hearers only."[7] Vigilance and effort are needed to keep the mind elevated. Act in accord with divine teachings, and be receptive through meditation and practicing the presence, and divine results will be forthcoming.

Lastly, I want to mention another form of attunement that I call receptive reading. With the development of subtle sensitivity, one can feel the consciousness of an author permeate his or her writing. That is why reading the works of a master can give practical inspiration as well as soul nourishment. Having extensively studied the writings of my spiritual master and other illumined souls, I can attest that this subtle benefit is one that goes beyond literary content and technical details. Even before beginning on my chosen path, I realized the truth of this claim. Browsing at a metaphysical store many years ago, I opened a book on Tibetan magic and was surprised to feel a strong oppressive force emanating from the text. In fact, it promptly gave me a headache. I then noticed a book by another Tibetan with whom I was not then familiar, the Dalai Lama. Wondering if I would have a similar experience from his text, I was pleased by the completely different outcome—waves of serenity engulfed me. My point is merely that energy, magnetism, and their impact on inner development are very real. Accepting these subtle realities and working in alignment with them can be of tremendous value to spiritual seekers and should be included in their efforts to progress.

10

Internalization: Expanding Awareness

E nergy and consciousness entering the body direct awareness out
through the senses into the material plane. The world becomes
revealed to us, but not God. This predicament causes an understandable, but inaccurate, identification of the seat of consciousness, the
soul, with its container, the body. To counter this delusion, outward-
flowing energy must be reversed and consciousness lifted. Accordingly,
we need to learn to withdraw or internalize those forces and focus them
on the centers of higher perception that reveal Spirit. Done properly,
subtle knots of energetic attachment are loosened, allowing increased
cognition of our innate divine nature and freedom from mortal identification. Internalization helps us realize these goals by emphasizing the
interior nature of spiritual realization: "The kingdom of God cometh not
with observation: Neither shall they say, Lo here! or, lo there! for, behold,
the kingdom of God is within you."[1]

To better understand this process, think in metaphorical terms. Imagine
shining a "flashlight of consciousness" so that we see wherever the light
beam is directed. Aimed through the senses, the world is revealed; turned
inside the body, its astral infrastructure becomes illumined. The mechan-
ics of this dynamic are rooted in the energy-consciousness relationship.
Wherever consciousness goes, energy flows with it, and vice versa.
Accordingly, when consciousness withdraws from the senses, as in sleep,
activating energy currents are disconnected, and sensory perceptions
cannot reach the brain. During such intervals, consciousness and energy

do not just disappear; they withdraw to function internally. As indicated, this condition occurs automatically in sleep. Energy retreats and outer awareness falls away. But slumber is a passive event that happens to us, and the descent of awareness into subconsciousness is not spiritually advantageous. To promote spiritual awakening we want to intentionally disconnect the senses and raise consciousness to superconscious planes where soul states are consciously perceived. That is the sole purpose of internalization and, eventually, meditation.

Focus must be pristine in spiritual matters for realizations to be unmarred. Just as lakes lose their mirrorlike reflective capability when agitated by wind, sense impressions distort mental clarity and compromise discernment. Internalizing awareness optimizes concentration and perception because it eliminates sense distractions and allows higher spiritual truths to be intuited pristinely. Materialists may find such matters irrelevant because sense-based activities are not subtle. For spiritual seekers, however, internalization is crucial because higher planes of reality are of a finer gradient. A properly internalized consciousness receives experiential proof of what might otherwise be esoteric theory and gains spiritual insights that could not be had otherwise.

An anecdote from the life and training of Swami Vivekananda shows the life-altering impact of genuine internalization. As previously mentioned, Vivekananda began his spiritual journey as a devout yet skeptical man. Saints seemed abundant in India, yet finding a fully illumined master was not easy, for, as the Bhagavad Gita states, "Out of thousands, one strives for spiritual attainment; and out of many blessed true seekers, who strive assiduously to reach Me, one, perhaps, perceives Me as I am."[2] After meeting Sri Ramakrishna and being told he was fully God-realized, Vivekananda still wanted proof. While the tentative mind's need for authentication is understandable, masters need not prove their stature to others unless inwardly directed to do so. And such was the case here. One day Sri Ramakrishna strolled among his disciples and lightly tapped Vivekananda. The latter immediately entered an ecstatic trance and became oblivious to the outer world. Turning to other nearby disciples,

Ramakrishna explained that Vivekananda was being given this exalted experience because he would not have it again until he remembered his identity as a sage descended from the Absolute and it was time to leave his body. Ramakrishna also remarked that Vivekananda had a significant mission to complete before departing the physical realm and that he held the key to Vivekananda's release. Needless to say, after returning to ordinary consciousness, Vivekananda was more convinced of Ramakrishna's high stature.

Inner experiences like these have an understandably profound effect. They open windows of perception to ordinarily inaccessible spiritual realities. Adepts may enter transcendent states at will, yet most of us require the aid of a master to do so. Masters serve as channels for divine grace to flow through and uplift readied souls. Lest anyone wonder, when an exalted experience is right for you, it will occur. If you are not ready, it will not. Do your best, and let results unfold in due course without attachment to outcomes. Spirit knows what is right for you along each step of your process.

Internalization is a skill that develops gradually and requires practice to master. Initial stages are characterized by deep relaxation during which the body feels heavy, limp, and completely at ease. This feeling is most often associated with semisleep states that commonly manifest between slumber and wakefulness. On the verge of sleep we can sense being cocooned inside the body, inhabiting it but not identified with it. This state is so tranquil that leaving it, for whatever reason, is undesirable. Movement brings energy to the limbs and wrests consciousness from its serene repose. The mood is simply ruined!

While semisubconscious experiences are enjoyable, superconscious states offer far more. When energy retreats deeper and is properly focused, body awareness is replaced by awareness of currents in the astral spine. Associated sensations can range from vast expansion to profound heaviness, physical dissolution, rising columns of energy, inner light, sound, subtle astral fragrances, extreme calmness, love, and heart-opening surges of joy. Such perceptions are not to be pursued for their own sake, nor are they necessarily significant of themselves. Rather, they substantiate that we are souls encased in multiple bodies, not just fleshy mortal beings. Let's now explore how to induce internalization.

Internalization Exercise

Closing the eyes cues the mind for sleep, but sleep causes passive sensory disconnection or unconscious internalization. For our purposes, we want to relax consciously at ever-deepening levels, yet remain fully alert. This requires keeping the closed eyes focused at the spiritual-eye center, which in turn elevates the mind toward superconsciousness.

The next two sequences help develop skillful withdrawal of energy and consciousness.

Sequence One: Withdrawing Energy

- Sit upright in a straight-backed chair or on a floor cushion.

- Close the eyes and gaze up into the spiritual eye.

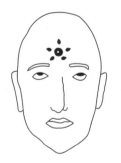

- Inhale through the nose for a count of eight, hold for eight, then exhale for eight. Do six times.

- Next, do a double-inhalation breath, short and long, through the nose.

- Hold the breath and gradually tense the body until it vibrates.

- Pay attention as energy floods the body (noticeable as tension).

- Now do a double-exhalation breath, short and long, through the mouth.

- Release all breath and release the muscles completely.

- Pay close attention to energy receding from the body (noticeable as relaxation).

- Repeat this double-breath sequence three times.

- Visualize streams of energy flowing back from the limbs to the spine. Feel.

- Repeat the double-breath sequence three more times.

- Focus again on energy retreating from the body periphery to the spine. Feel.

- Drop body awareness and focus on being centered in the spine.

Sequence Two: Withdrawing Consciousness

- Assume a straight-spine posture with closed eyes upturned to the spiritual eye.

- Visualize yourself as falling asleep.

- Feel the sensation of letting go, but remain alert and focused at the spiritual eye.

- Let each breath take you deeper inside the body core.

- Disregard all sensory signals as every current of attention turns inward.

- Dive increasingly deeper, away from the external world.

- Float in an inner bubble of peace.

- Melt and dissolve into a serene state of "just being."

- Absorbed deeply within, you can become completely oblivious to the world.

Develop the sense of withdrawing into and being centered in the spine. Hold that feeling even when returning to engage the world. Sit, move, and breathe with relaxed inward poise; you will feel more physically and emotionally balanced by doing so.

From a yogic perspective, internalization is as vital to developing inner awareness as breathing is to ordinary life. It is not a relative matter; it is the way things work. Just as one cannot go swimming without entering water, you cannot approach divine realms without going within. The material world is forever external; the realm of Spirit is internal. Yet not everyone who pursues spiritual growth embraces inner experience. Some fear it, thinking the subtle landscape is rife with delusional forces. Others prefer doing charitable works or facilitating various outer rituals. Although such activities can be beneficial, they do not of themselves produce Self-realization. This observation brings us back to internalization. Taking inner development seriously necessitates adhering to scientific, reproducible methods that foster genuine growth. I stress this point now because significant spiritual matters are being addressed. When people find themselves at such junctures, contrary influences, habits, or thoughts often arise to challenge their fortitude. Such patterns were referenced earlier, yet revisiting the subject reminds us of this reality and the need for vigilance. Otherwise, the unwary or conflicted person may find inner efforts dislodged by the buffeting storms of delusion. Here is an example of what I mean.

Before a former student of mine moved out of state, she had attended my meditation, chanting, and hatha classes regularly and with keen enthusiasm. She found in them a healing balm for her otherwise chaotic life. Seeking to soften her imminent transition, I provided several books to give spiritual sustenance. Several weeks later I ran into her husband, who had returned to town briefly on a business trip. Inquiring about his wife, I learned she was having difficulty following the spiritual practices she formerly found so favorable. As I understand it, she kept wondering, "Why make a spiritual effort now? If we reincarnate, why not enjoy myself fully until I am more in the mood?" Despite my efforts at long-distance counseling, disciplined inner development lost the battle to fruits of the moment. My former student's dilemma has afflicted many earnest seekers. "The harvest truly is plenteous, but the labourers are few."[3] In fact, a similar conflict reputedly inspired the earthy prayer of Saint Augustine of Hippo, who beseeched the Lord, "Grant me chastity and continency, but not yet."[4]

Struggles between body and soul are classic and unavoidable: They stem from our being part flesh and part Spirit. Soul aspirations clash with bodily desires until the conflict is resolved by wisdom. Most people indulge in outer caprice for ages until the ego realizes its folly. Even knowing better, many individuals are so attached to sensory gratification that it takes repeated poundings of misfortune, frustration, and disillusionment before genuine readiness for change takes root. Past habits and desires continue to wrestle for dominance even then. Internalization plays a key role in this shift by introducing us to spiritual states that are more gratifying than sense pleasures. As a nexus to higher awareness, it gives a basis of comparison that reconfigures perceptions of joy from outer reference points to inner ones. By doing so, it fortifies resolve to abandon addictive sensory deception. Without that basis, primal temptations would be overpowering.

Mixed messages are abundant in the discussion of senses versus Spirit. For some, this perception of a conflict is inaccurate and stifling of whole-person integration. From my experience, however, we must learn to spiritualize everything and accept paradox. Like it or not, there are aspects of universal creation that are delusional and must be known as such, because that is the way things are. As long as you are asleep, every dream seems real until you waken. A similar play of divine consciousness perpetuates the dream of creation and the false sense of separation from Spirit. Only through direct insight do we awaken and realize the

Divine Singularity. So, we must learn to acknowledge ourselves as both matter and spirit. We must abide by the rules of creation but realize that we are fundamentally more than it. Our engagement with the material realm changes as we grow in understanding and learn that the objective world is not a final reality but the creative display of Spirit; we begin to look past it to the enduring spiritual source that created it.

The good news is that the stranglehold of sense snares can be broken by elevation in divine communion. Lesser desires are gradually neutralized when the heart is aflame with love of God and we realize that our hunger for fulfillment can genuinely be sated within. Although such states may take a while to cultivate and stabilize, patient persistence pays off. Even small steps forward are significant, as each stride builds faith for the next. Make continued efforts until good habits replace bad ones and internal conditions become enduring. Do not be discouraged if you fall or err against your will. Get up and try again. Stay the course. Take solace from Yogananda's counsel that saints are merely sinners who never give up. And as his guru, Sri Yukteswar, similarly advised, "Forget the past. . . . The vanished lives of all men are dark with many shames. Human conduct is ever unreliable until anchored in the Divine. Everything in future will improve if you are making a spiritual effort now."[5]

11

The Art of Developing Concentration

Skills are usually considered to be acquired traits, unlike natural talent. Yet even talent can be improved on and become extraordinary through proper training and refinement. Our next step of developing concentration is no exception. Some consider it the by-product of a solid work ethic or the reflection of innate character; others feel it arises automatically by focusing on whatever is at hand. Both ideas have merit, yet neither examines the underlying nature of concentration and, accordingly, how it can be reliably honed. Those who lack concentration can acquire it; those with an inherent ability can improve what they already possess.

What precisely is concentration? It is the power to withdraw mental awareness from objects of distraction and place it uninterruptedly on a select item or idea. It is developed and enhanced by learning to eradicate objects of distraction and then directing pristine perception intentionally in a one-pointed manner. What are objects of distraction? These consist of sensory impressions plus the related thoughts and memories they beget. How can the mind be freed from objects of distraction? Through energy control and internalization. The importance of both is illustrated here:

Imagine having an important work assignment due tomorrow. Entering your study, you close the door and start formulating an action plan. The phone rings; you ignore it. Nothing is going to disturb you. Everything is going fine, but the room feels stuffy so you crack a window. Now you hear the neighbor kids playing basketball; they are making a racket but certainly having fun. You momentarily drift and recall some of your own earlier pickup games, particularly the time you had to play against that gorgeous tomboy! Isn't life funny? Who knew the two of you would eventually get married? And what an amazing honeymoon in the Caimans! So it goes . . .

This entire scenario unfurled from just two sense impressions, feeling and hearing. All the subsequent thoughts were an ungoverned sequence of reactions. Imagine how we respond to sights, smells, and tastes, too! In short, the senses must be mastered to keep the mind in check. Otherwise we are constantly subject to the symphony of impressions and associated memories they evoke. To understand how such control is accomplished, recall the main principle discussed in the chapter on internalization: Sensory perceptions are temporarily disengaged when energy is withdrawn from the body in deep relaxation. This tenet is imperative for sense management and, consequently, for developing concentration. Pause for a moment to acknowledge what we have learned thus far and appreciate the interrelated factors that promote spiritual growth. Everything is energetic and is of Spirit. Understanding and applying the principles that govern this cosmology foster optimal spiritual realization, regardless of one's faith tradition. As simple as this tenet may sound, it is profound. The mystery of creation and learning how to attain union with the Creator are not matters of idle speculation. They are the stuff of inner science and direct realization.

Let's further our process by examining more advanced aspects of internalization and concentration.

CONTROLLING THE HEART: GOVERNING THE SENSE MECHANISM

Ancient yogis observed that life force descends from the brain through the heart, then into the sensory-motor nerves. These, in turn, report and respond to the external world. Systematic relaxation reverses energy currents from the muscles and, to a significant degree, the sensory motor system. But more is required to completely disengage the senses and induce superior interiorization. Withdrawal of energy must be extended to include the heart, through which energy flows in the first place. The way to achieve this is simple and yet extremely effective: watching the breath. Cardiopulmonary functions are intimately connected, and, as such, breath patterns have reciprocal impact on heart activity. Passive yet deliberate observation of the breath has the effect of calming the heart, especially when done in conjunction with certain techniques. As the heart rate lessens, the energy pouring into the heart reverses course, withdraws back to the astral spine, and flows upward to the brain. At this juncture the sensory-motor nerves become disconnected, freeing us to concentrate fully without disturbances arising from external sense impressions.

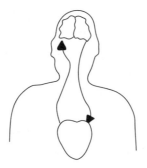

Breathing is necessary for physiological processes. Oxygen intake serves to change waste-bearing venous blood into vitalized arterial blood and to provide energy for the body. The waste matter is derived from metabolic functions that axiomatically produce cell decay. When metabolic activity is high, venous blood production rises, as does the need for oxygen to cleanse the system. Likewise, as metabolic toxins are reduced, less venous blood is created; oxygen requirements decrease, and we breathe less. If no such waste is produced, respiration can stop, at least temporarily. For this halt to occur, cellular decay must be suspended—a feat achieved with pure diet, halting bodily motion, and stilling the heart. A related technique that quiets the heart will be taught, but before doing so, several essential points should be revisited or highlighted.

Improper eating pollutes the system, requires excess energy to digest, and keeps the mind body-bound. Proper diet and periodic fasting eliminate impurities and free energy for higher applications.

Sound has power. Certain pitches can shatter glass, yet sonic technology also has subtle applications that can enhance spiritual pursuits. Certain tones calm the heart and lungs when made in conjunction with watching the breath and physical stillness. These sound phenomena form the basis for complete interiorization and concentration.

Movement is natural and a hallmark of life, yet is also a prime generator of metabolic waste. Stillness achieved by deep, systematic relaxation can significantly reduce cellular decay and decreases the need for blood purification. Corresponding heart and lung activity lessen as metabolic waste drops. Heart and lung actions can stop completely in states of advanced calmness. Rather than cause death, this condition of superrelaxation gives rise to a conscious breathless state in which energy is redistributed throughout the body, vitalizing and sustaining it on a subtle level. The great rest that complete cessation of movement, internally and externally, gives the body adds to its vitality when active, can enhance longevity, and enriches the capacity for subtle inner perception while meditating.

Some spiritual adepts can forgo eating, breathing, or other common life functions for extended periods—sometimes indefinitely—because they have mastered living solely by life force. Jesus referred to this condition by declaring, "Man shall not live by bread alone, but by every word that proceedeth out of the mouth of God."[1] The "mouth of God" is the medulla oblongata, through which cosmic energy enters the body, and the "word" is vibrating cosmic life force. Examples from different faiths include Giri Bala, an Indian woman saint who did not eat or drink for fifty-six years, and Saint Therese Neumann, a Catholic stigmatic who lived for years on one communion wafer daily; the communion wafer, incidentally, had to be consecrated or she could not swallow it. Another is Sadhu Haridas, who agreed to be buried for four months, was disinterred and declared dead, then reanimated himself. More details of these episodes are found in Yogananda's *Autobiography of a Yogi*. The main point in mentioning them is to underscore the unusual spectrum of reality that inhabits the spiritual domain and the range of faiths that such feats span. Paranormal living can seem relatively normal whenever divine consciousness is involved.

Sound and Vibration

Use of sound frequencies deliberately exercised for spiritual purposes is rarely employed in the West outside of Wiccan or indigenous traditions. In Eastern Vedic cultures, such concepts and practices compose an ancient esoteric science called mantra. Governed by the laws of physics and metaphysics, the basis for mantra is in the nature of creation. As we discussed, everything is formed of increasingly dense arrays of vibration and, in turn, each vibration produces corresponding frequencies of sound and light. As specific chemicals combine to make select compounds, certain tonal formulas may be voiced aloud or mentally to cause definite results. Mantras are specific word or sound sets that can be harnessed to manipulate matter or consciousness in precise ways. For our purposes, the science of mantra is used to calm breath and heart, reduce cell decay, focus the mind, and induce concentration.

The concentration mantra that Yogananda taught, "Hong Sau," is alternately called "So Hum" or "Hum Sa" in other yogic systems. The words loosely translate as "I am He" or "I am Spirit" and, interestingly, are connected to the title Paramahansa, which means "Highest Swan":

Lit., *parama*, highest; *hansa*, swan. The white swan is mythologically represented as the vehicle or mount of Brahma the Creator. The sacred *hansa*, said to have the power of extracting only milk from a mixture of milk and water, is thus a symbol of spiritual discrimination.

Ahan-sa or *'han-sa* (pronounced *hong-sau*) is literally "I am He." These potent Sanskrit syllables possess a vibratory connection with the incoming and the outgoing breath. Thus with his every breath man unconsciously asserts the truth of his being: *I am He!*[2]

How to Practice

Use of this mantra requires that it be repeated in conjunction with breath. The method involved is to mentally repeat the first sound, Hong, while inhaling and to mentally repeat the second sound, Sau, while exhaling. Eyes remain closed and lifted to the spiritual-eye center during inhalation, exhalation, and associated practice time.

Some preliminary points to remember are:

- Breath and mind react to one another. As the breath flows, so goes the mind.

- The mind becomes balanced and calm by concentrating on and quieting the breath.

- The Hong Sau mantra augments this process by inducing a pure, focused state.

The following step-by-step outline spells out how to proceed.

The Hong Sau Concentration Technique

1. Sit straight and place the hands with palms upturned on the lap at the juncture of the torso and thighs. If this feels awkward, rest the hands

in any comfortable position. What is essential is to keep relaxed and maintain a straight spine.

2. Close the eyes and gently lift the gaze to the spiritual-eye center between the eyebrows. If easier, keep the eyes half open, but again, gaze upward into the spiritual eye. Do not strain.

3. Offer a silent prayer to Spirit for aid and guidance in your efforts.

4. Do the following breath and energy-control technique to calm the mind:

Inhale through the nose for a count of twelve. Imagine drawing in peace, calm, or joy with each breath.

Hold the breath for a count of twelve. Bathe the mind and nerves in stillness.

Exhale through the nose for a count of twelve. Release all negativity and anxiety. Go deeper within.

Repeat this cycle six to twelve times.

5. Now tense and release as follows to relax the body:

Double-inhale: take a short breath followed by a long breath in through the nose. Hold the breath and tense the body until it vibrates.

Double-exhale: release a short breath followed by a long breath out through the mouth. Simultaneously relax the body completely. This technique also helps rid the system of excess carbon, a metabolic waste by-product.

Relax physically, mentally, and emotionally. Feel yourself becoming heavy and still.

Repeat three to six times.

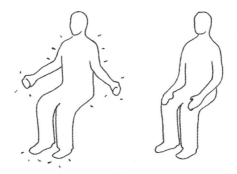

6. Now, inhale fully through the nose and exhale fully through the mouth.

   Forget about counting or controlling the breath.

   All further breathing should be done solely through the nose.

7. With the next inhale (nose) mentally repeat the sound HONG (rhymes with song). During exhalation (nose) mentally repeat the sound SAU (saw). Continue the breath and mantra pattern, repeating the mantra mentally only. Do not move the lips or tongue.

8. Observe your breath rhythms with inner awareness. Remain an impartial witness, not caring whether the breath flows in or out or remains quiet. Do not control it in any way. Just keep repeating the mantra in conjunction with the breath.

9. Focus on the pauses that arise naturally as breathing slows. Enjoy these tranquil spaces. Melt into them. Continue using the mantra as prescribed when respiration resumes.

   Practice passive observation: Never forcibly hold the breath.

10. If the mind wanders, gently bring it back to repeating Hong or Sau. If inner gaze placement drifts, gently redirect it to the spiritual eye.

    Remember to keep the spine straight, body relaxed, and eyes uplifted.

I recommend beginning with fifteen to thirty minutes of Hong Sau twice daily. Do less if that seems excessive, but keep fifteen minutes per session in mind as a good introductory goal. Do more if you like. Significant results will not come from fitful efforts; regularity, depth, and enjoyment are necessary. Going deep is more important than length of practice, yet combining depth with length yields optimal outcomes.

The time following practice is a valuable period for absorbing the peaceful aftereffects of what you have just done. Be still and feel. Calm, interiorized receptivity develops intuition, and holding to inner states helps one to spiritualize one's life. Resuming activity too quickly without holding to these aftereffects is like spilling a bucket of peace. This time is also ideal for prayer. If so inclined, pray to God in the language of your heart—nothing artificial or scripted. Continue praying deeply until a profound calmness comes over you or an increasing joy fills the heart. Then resume stillness, and let yourself receive whatever Spirit sends to the inner sanctum of your soul.

More about Prayer

Knowledge of prayer is relevant, so let's address the subject a bit further. Prayer is a common practice yet also a relatively misunderstood one. Those who question the effectiveness of prayer do not grasp that it, too, is governed by subtle laws. The spiritual-eye center is a seat of higher awareness and concentration and a locus for broadcasting thought. Like any transmitting and receiving equipment, the mind must be attuned properly to operate well. An unfocused mental state cannot issue prayers effectively, nor can it receive subtle responses. Attention must be one-pointed and calm to transmit prayers with potent force and to accurately intuit divine feedback. Spirit receives all prayers, yet responds to those made viable by right method. Again, the key to its success is that the mind must be correctly focused for prayer to work.

Another tip is to be persistent. Do not quit after a few cursory attempts. Remain steadfast until you feel a profound calmness or joy, indicators that your efforts have been received. And have faith: "Therefore I say unto you, What things soever ye desire, when ye pray, believe that ye receive them, and ye shall have them."[3] God answers, albeit often mysteriously and not in an anticipatable timeline or manner. Responses will come in due course, so stay receptive. Even if they are not immediate, be open to life circumstances through which answers manifest. "Pray to thy Father which is in secret; and thy Father which seeth in secret shall reward thee openly [on the material plane]."[4] Take note of these things and be appreciative. Gratitude opens the doors through which abundance can flow.

Prayers should be unsophisticated and heartfelt. Language is less important than feeling. Saint Francis repeated "My God and my all" until Jesus materialized to him. Yogananda advocated prayer demands like "Come to me!" "Be Thou mine!" or "Reveal Thyself!" to reinforce soul intimacy with Spirit as opposed to a distant, beggar consciousness. Prayer works regardless of approach but, again, requires patience, persistence, and faith. For those interested in such activities, various kinds of prayer associated with healing have been explored in the book *Healing Words: The Power of Prayer and the Practice of Medicine* by Larry Dossey. It is a groundbreaking book that integrates Western science, medical research, and spiritual practice.

Returning to matters at hand, the benefit of a valid concentration technique cannot be stressed enough. Although viable for many reasons, its supreme impact is on the ego. Scientific concentration induces a breathless state that prompts the ego to realize its existence as pure awareness independent of breath and body. Weaned from primal physical associations, the ego finally begins to know its enduring nature and reality as soul, an aspect of eternal consciousness. With the stranglehold of mortal limitation weakened, the ego is fortified to overcome its delusive separation from the Divine.

Here is a basic review and impact of the mantra concentration technique:

- Hong Sau calms the mind and stills the breath.

- It loosely translates to mean "I am He" or "I am That [Spirit]."

- Correct use slows the metabolism, causing energy to withdraw from the body and heart and to be routed to the brain, thereby disconnecting sensory-motor nerves from external engagement.

- As sensory impulses recede, so do related distractions (thoughts and memories).

- Attention, now freed, can be concentrated.

- Temporary breath cessation lets the ego recollect its soul essence.

- Consciousness realizes that it alone endures.

These things have an undeniable impact on spiritual awakening, yet can lead one to ask if a particular mantra technique is necessary. Various teachers use similar mantras, some of which I have already mentioned. I teach the Hong Sau method because it is what I am familiar with and because it is part of a comprehensive system taught by a genuine spiritual master. Yogananda used the technique because it lacks ambiguity and entails no happenstance or circuitous process. The mantra, mode of practice, and outcomes are precise, reproducible, and time-tested. It is a clear way to achieve mental states linked to larger spiritual perspectives. And it is inclusive: the metaphysical principles involved are not for one religion alone but are applicable within any faith tradition.

Not all focusing techniques are equally effective. Concentration as outlined thus far is a matter of subtle science, not an incidental by-product. All that has been shared to this point would be meaningless were it less than as represented. To foster pristine concentration is why the Hong Sau mantra was developed. It is an intricate yet easy modality that works in a safe, reliable way. Other methods could very well deliver comparable results, but a scientific technique, practiced properly and with full attention, must undoubtedly yield optimal results.

My perspective is admittedly born of bias and experience. As a teenager, I began meditating yet hadn't the foggiest notion of what I was doing. My martial arts training included mental-centering exercises, but they were vague. Given my inclinations, I experimented and found that a profoundly still state could be achieved if I sat with closed eyes and silently repeated the word *peace* with each inhale, then *calm* with every exhale. (This practice is very similar to the mantra routine just shared.) I also noted the process grew richer when done frequently. From this I concluded that if a self-taught practice was beneficial, proper training in a genuine spiritual technique should be superior.

My assumption proved largely correct. After receiving formal meditation instruction, I found it offered considerably more substance than untutored practice. Then I hit a snag. As mentioned earlier, Herbert Benson conducted a meditation study in the 1960s resulting in his book *The Relaxation Response.* He proved that conscious, passively alert inhalation and exhalation coupled with select focus words induced a physiologic state called the relaxation response (what I had discovered accidently)—the opposite of the stress-induced flight-or-fight response. While appreciative of these findings, I felt that his work threatened what I had learned about mantra by suggesting that random word formulas were equally effective. Here is where my bias entered in: If the mantra was irrelevant, then the scientific basis for yoga plus the effort I spent learning it could easily be questioned. Fortunately, a form of vindication was at hand. In a subsequent book, *Beyond the Relaxation Response,* Benson discovered that word sets of a spiritual nature had a more profound impact on practitioners than did neutral choices. Furthermore, inclusion of a sacred framework provided a greater sense of the holy in their daily lives than did secular practices. Whether this result was a placebo effect or not did not fundamentally matter; the results displayed enhanced outcomes sufficient to merit my trust in the processes learned thus far. Despite jitters about justifying time in the yoga trenches, it is never inappropriate to question. Blind belief in anything, be it technique or a master, is not the same as faith born of experience. In the pursuit of truth, we must be willing to challenge assumptions, no matter how precious, yet cling to truth devotedly when revealed.

Benson's continued explorations of science and metaphysics took him to the Himalayas, where he was introduced to an esoteric skill called Ta Mo, or internal fire. Like mantra, this energy-control technique evolved from Eastern meditative disciplines; it involved generating inner heat to withstand frigid mountain temperatures. As an amusing aside, some monks who trained in Ta Mo had what could only be called "wet-blanket contests." In a monkish spirit of fun, they stripped to their loincloths while exposed to subfreezing cold. Layers of wet blankets would be heaped on them, and whoever dried the largest number of blankets by inner heat quickest won the competition.

Clearly, methods of energy control exist in many forms and for multiple reasons. Nevertheless, the mantra technique provided in this chapter is a worthy skill that delivers its purpose: concentration.

Some people feel guarded about mantras for a variety of reasons. If you are one of these, use generic focus words as I once did. Your initial practice may be more akin to a neutral relaxation-response approach, but it is a worthy start. Try incorporating sacred words or phrases you feel at ease with for potentially better and more meaningful results. Remember, the goal of meditation and the practices provided here is to help you seek, and realize, the kingdom within. Holy words used in mantra-like fashion can deepen focus on the Divine. For example, the Eastern Orthodox Church has a meditative exercise that involves repeating "Lord Jesus Christ" with each inhale and "Have mercy on me" during exhalation. Ultimately, you must work with what best suits you, because if a practice is not endorsed inwardly, it will not be used or useful.

Here is a list of mantras and alternate word sets for easy reference. If none appeal, make up your own. All of these practices should be done with the breathing rhythms described thus far. With the inhale, mentally repeat the sound(s)/word(s) in the left column; with the exhale, repeat the sound(s) in the right column.

Concentration Mantras

Hong	Sau
Hum	Sa
So	Hum

Secular Focus Words

Peace	Calm
Love	Joy
Let	Go

Christian

Hail	Mary
Jesus	Christ
Lord Jesus Christ	Have mercy on me/us

Jewish

Sha	lom (Peace)
Has	hem (the Name)
Sh'ma	Yisroel (Hear, O Israel)

Islamic

Allah	Be Praised
	Is Merciful

Tibetan Buddhist

Om	Mani Padme Hum

Hindu

Om	Shanti
Hare	Krishna/Rama
Jai	Shiva

12

Meditation: Absorption in Spirit

A ll we have covered in this book up to now has led to this point: meditation. What precisely is meditation? Meditation is not, as some believe, a passive process of blanking the mind, concentrated activity, or philosophical pondering. It is a very specific art and science of reuniting the soul with Infinite Spirit, or God. As such it is central to the spiritual life and pivotal to attaining Self-realization.

The distinction between meditation and concentration is one of context and degree. People can concentrate on anything, but meditation, in our framework, is concentration used solely to know God. When people initially practice meditation, their minds are mostly attempting to achieve a fixed status. In such conditions, traces of ego remain, a sense of "I" that keeps the soul slightly separate from the object of contemplation, Spirit. True meditation occurs when ego consciousness is fully dissolved, thus freeing the soul to complete absorption in the Absolute.

Remember that in an incarnate soul, energy and consciousness enter at the medulla oblongata. From there they go to the brain and are routed to the chakras, the centers of light and life in the astral spine. These forces course throughout the body, sustaining life and activating the senses. Awareness pouring through the senses reveals the world to us, but not God. As a result, after the soul has been in a physical form overly long, it forgets its real nature and identifies with the body as ego. Scientific meditation shatters this hypnotic delusion. By reversing the outward, matter-oriented flow of life force and consciousness, the senses can be disconnected from outer perceptions and awareness singularly focused at the centers of spiritual perception in the brain. Ego awareness is transmuted into intuitive insight by further concentration and right technique. The soul recalls its immortal nature and awakens in oneness with Spirit. This process yields increasing peace and bliss until, in highest meditative states, all separation from God dissolves. Consciousness becomes immersed in the Divine within and beyond creation. At this juncture, the goal of all spiritual pursuits—alternatively called nirvikalpa samadhi, salvation, enlightenment, liberation, returning to the source, or cosmic consciousness—has been achieved. The prodigal soul child returns to its Heavenly Father and "shall go no more out."[1]

The ultimate state of meditation may sound beyond reach, but it actually reflects our truest nature: Spirit. It is our birthright and why we need not seek to become something spiritual but to grasp what we already are: Divine. In the Buddhist tradition, what is deemed holy and latent in all is called Buddha nature. Its radiant presence is covered only by a veil of ignorance. Meditation is essentially the art and science of revealing our innate perfection.

A question arises whether concentration of itself leads to meditation or whether further techniques are needed. Both are true, since the distinction between meditation and concentration is one of context and degree. Consider the analogy of a magnifying glass, in which light is narrowed to a beam of burning intensity. The gathering of one-pointed mental force is concentration. Unswerving focus changes into meditation once the light of awareness dissolves the ego and consciousness merges into the object of concentration. In our process, we first employ a concentration technique to focus the mind and then direct the focused mind on Spirit using a secondary meditation technique. The meditation method provided here harnesses attunement of consciousness with an aspect of the Divine. Given that framework, let's briefly review attunement fundamentals before proceeding into actual technique instruction.

Attunement was described earlier as establishing an exact vibratory affinity with a person, thing, or quality that fosters an identical state with it. If you take two tuning forks of similar frequency and activate one then hold it to the other, the second will start vibrating at a corresponding rate. Being harmonically attuned, the two reflect each other precisely and emit duplicate sounds. Loved ones can periodically read each other's minds, since their at-one-ment is so refined that they can briefly share one mind and discern the other's thoughts. In spiritual matters, this principle of attunement is vital. Whoever follows a master or divine teaching seeks to emulate the master or the teaching. Along with personal spiritual effort, attunement in such sacred relationships channels vibrations to disciples, which helps lift their untutored consciousnesses to higher states.

Meditation on Spirit applies these precepts to a particular aspect of God. The precise aspect of Spirit one chooses to harmonize with depends on personal preference and relevant technique. The eight classical attributes of Spirit are light, love, wisdom, peace, power, joy, calmness, and sound. The meditation technique that Yogananda taught and I share here is part of a traditional practice called Nada yoga. It focuses on attunement to Spirit via its aspect of primal sound. The technique is safe and soothing, and it facilitates immense spiritual realization. It is a profound method with many layers of benefit.

The divine sound is not to be confused with traditional notes of a tonal scale. It is the cosmic reverberation variously known as Om, Aum, Hum, Amen, or Amin. In the Christian tradition, it is referred to as the Word. The significance of the Word is its link to creation. As previously explained, from Spirit arose a prime impulse to create. Initial manifestations of creation were projected as thought, whose nature is vibration. Thus, the original creative expression was the Word, or cosmic vibration, with its inherent qualities of light and sound. The saint Shams-i-Tabriz commented about the sacred sound, "The universe was manifested out of the Divine Sound; from It came into being the Light."[2] His disciple, the famous mystical poet Rumi, similarly commented, "Seek the Sound that never ceases, seek the sun that never sets."[3] Both refer to the primal aspects of creation and attunement with the Creator through these aspects.

Being of Spirit, cosmic sound is eternal and omnipresent. Ever-present yet invisible, it is called the Holy Spirit and is filled with a divine intelligence known by Christians as Christ Consciousness or by Hindus as Tat/Kutastha Chaitanya. Notice the dual-faith Holy Trinity model. Christians hold to a Father, Son, and Holy Spirit construct, while in Vedic teaching the same elements are referred to as Sat, Tat, and Om. Very simply, God is One but manifests as three: Creator, Cosmic Energy, and Divine Intelligence. The universal nature of this triad is referenced in the following compilation of Taoist passages:

Before the earth in space was spun,
Beneath the heaven's feet,
There was a mighty spirit, One,
Calm, wondrous, complete.

Changeless, yet moving; from its womb
All things came into birth;

This is the mystic bride and groom,
Maker of heaven and earth.

Something there is, whose veiled creation was
Before the earth or sky began to be;
So silent, so aloof, and so alone,
It changes not, nor fails, but touches all:
Conceive it as the Mother of the world.
I do not know its name;
A name for it is "Way";

The Way begot one,
And the one, two;
And the two begot three
And three, all else.[4]

The Christian and Vedic frameworks displayed below have references specific to both cultures. The terms may differ, but the ideas remain identical.

Holy Trinity

Sat/Father	Tat/Son	Om/Holy Ghost
The Transcendent Truth/Bliss/Consciousness (God in and beyond Creation)	Christ/Krishna Kuthastha Chaitanya (Guiding, Divine Intelligence)	Amen/The Word (Creative Vibratory Force)

God is omnipresent, and the soul, being part of God, is omnipresent in potential. The body, which houses the soul, is reducible to organs, tissues, chemicals, cells, molecules, atoms, electrons, protons, etc. Further reduction reveals vital forces, sensations, will, and gradations of consciousness. While the human form appears distinct, it is composed of primal cosmic essence, divine thought. As a glacier is solid but joins the sea when melted, so does the body—which is fashioned from cosmic consciousness—resume cosmic stature when the consciousness that infuses it merges into its source. This truth is realized through correct meditation. "As seed planted in proper soil brings forth a tree, so from proper meditation instilled in the soul, consciousness of omnipresence will manifest."[5]

COSMIC SOUND

Sounds roam the airways undetected except by relevant apparatus like radio. The human body is equipped to hear the Om because our chakras emit distinct sounds when consciousness and energy flow through them. More specifically, the Om vibration, or variations of it, can be discerned using a specific meditation technique that directs awareness from the senses toward the tonal frequencies of the chakras. Om is associated with the spiritual-eye center, the sixth chakra, and revealed when attention is rightly fixed there. However, hearing the Om sound only occasionally is not sufficient. As the nature of true meditation is to become absorbed in the object of concentration, we must merge into the Om vibration and expand with it beyond the confines of the finite body into omnipresence. When we truly meditate on Om, we can become Spirit-as-the-Word throughout creation.

Given the relationship between creation and the holy intelligence governing it, advanced states of union with the Word open us to receive the Son/Tat/Christ Consciousness that infuses It. Once that has been attained, we become able to unite with the Absolute Transcendent Spirit beyond creation. This is the esoteric meaning of ascending to the Father through the Son. Contrary to popular theology, that ascension has nothing to do with the person of Jesus or any other savior. It means we all must return to our source in a step-by-step fashion that proceeds and culminates in an identical manner for everyone. While it is true that the means or paths toward achieving union with Spirit may vary, none are exempt from the cosmic realities that underlie this process. That is why a scientific understanding and approach to soul emancipation is a blessing; it provides true insight and means to gain Realization regardless of faith orientation.

The Sounds of Silence

Two things provided here should help readers appreciate the universal nature of this inner sound technique: three Christian and Judaic verses referencing the chakras plus a chart with additional information. The verses are not intended to overlay Eastern concepts on Western paradigms, but to show metaphysically consistent allegories. Each image has an explanation provided to help the interpretive process. Many biblical verses, particularly in Revelation, complement esoteric Vedic teaching.

> And [the angel] said unto me, What seest thou? And I said, I have looked, and behold a candlestick all of gold [the sushumna or central astral channel], with a bowl [the crown chakra] upon the top of it, and his seven lamps [the seven chakras] thereon.[6]

Thou wast upon the holy mountain of God [height of inner attainment]; thou hast walked up and down in the midst of the stones of fire [ascended and descended the astral spinal channel and chakras].[7]

I was in the Spirit on the Lord's day [raised into spiritual ecstasy], and heard behind me a great voice, as of a trumpet [OM vibration]. . . .
And I turned to see the voice that spake with me. And being turned, I saw seven golden candlesticks [chakras].[8]

Much information about chakras is accessible online or in books. This chart is meant solely to present their qualities, locations, Vedic names, and, most importantly, sounds as taught by Yogananda and other Eastern authorities. As mentioned previously, Om is associated with the sixth chakra, the seat of divine perception.

Chakra Chart

Order	Vedic Name	Quality	Location	Sound
1st Chakra	Muladhara	Coccyx	Earth	Bumblebee
2nd Chakra	Svadishthana	Genital	Water	Flute
3rd Chakra	Manipura	Navel	Fire	Harp
4th Chakra	Anahata	Dorsal/Heart	Air	Gong/Bell
5th Chakra	Vishuddha	Cervical	Ether	Rushing Waters
6th Chakra	Ajna	Spiritual Eye	Super-Ether	OM
7th Chakra	Sahasrara	Crown	Spirit	

Inner Sound Meditation Technique

To meditate on inner sounds, and the Om vibration in particular, one must first learn how to hear them. Now is the time to do so.

1. Sit erect with the spine straight and body relaxed.

2. Begin with a prayer to God/Spirit.

3. Practice a concentration technique such as Hong Sau until the breath is calm and the mind is interiorized. Ten minutes will do to start.

4. Place your elbows on a support, such as a meditation elbow rest or tabletop with a firm cushion on it. Be able to bring your thumbs to the ears without leaning forward or curving the spine.

5. Press the thumbs comfortably but firmly over each tragus to close the ear. (The tragus is the flap of cartilage located at each ear opening.)

6. Place the little fingers lightly on the closed eyelids near the outer corners—and on the eye sockets—to gently hold the eyelids down and keep the eyeballs still. The right little finger secures the right eye, as the left little finger does the left eye.

7. Rest the other fingers on the forehead, pointing inward to the spiritual eye. Imagine them magnetically directing energy to that center.

8. Gaze into the spiritual eye with closed eyes and mentally chant Om, Om, Om at that center. Make no audible sound or movement of the tongue.

9. Listen calmly but intently inside the right ear. Astral sounds—particularly those of the chakras—are heard loudest here.

10. Concentrate on whatever inner sound you hear, be it physical (e.g., the heartbeat) or astral.

11. Focus on the loudest sound.

12. Keep gazing into the spiritual eye and chanting Om automatically.

13. Simultaneously remain listening for the Om sound. After a period you can try to see the spiritual eye, but that is not a priority.

14. If you hear Om right away (a great roaring sound like the ocean), do not listen for other sounds; concentrate solely on it. Try to become one with and expand in Om.

Key Points

- Use an armrest. This supports the arm and hand positions plus eliminates muscular strain.

- Do not lean on the hands or tense the body. Remain upright and relaxed.

- Use soft ear plugs to block outer sounds if your ears are too sensitive for touch.

- Keep focused on whatever inner sound is loudest in the right ear.

- The sounds you should be attending to are of a subtle astral nature.

- For best results, practice regularly and, occasionally, for extended periods.

Review Tips

Always try to hear the Om vibration, though this might not happen immediately. That is okay. Pay attention to whatever inner sound you hear most clearly. It could be the breath, heartbeat, high-pitched tones of the astral body, or sounds of other chakras. As indicated in the chart, the latter are the bumblebee, flute, harp, gong/bell, rushing waters, or Om. Any of them is fine and a step along the way. Let each sound take you to another level, yet do not strain or try to bypass anything.

Simply follow the sound trail. Eventually you will hear the Om. Do not feel that you are finished after you have done so. Just as it takes more than listening to Mozart to play his music, it takes more than sporadic hearing of Om to merge into Spirit. You have to resonate with, merge into, and increase with it. Om reveals itself progressively through bodily vibrations, then expansion of consciousness. The quality of your experience will unfold naturally according to capacity and receptivity. The key to success is regular, attentive practice. Remember, depth of focus plus length of immersion provides best results. As spiritual growth is neither a race nor a contest, seeking outcomes only creates tension. Just practice the technique and enjoy the process. Your development will come in due course from relaxed, sustained, devotional effort.

You have been given a scientific, spiritually valid meditation technique. Now it is imperative that you use it. The information in this book provides principles and procedures based on cosmic laws to accelerate spiritual growth, yet, again, it is up to you to make the effort. Nothing external—scripture, ritual, or belief—can replace direct perception of Spirit. Achieving that requires patient discipline harnessed to right technique and attitude. Divine illumination *is* attainable by following the methods put forth herein.

The Personal Impact of Meditation

While I would love to pop up like a piece of toast and say, "I am perfect now!" the simple truth is that I make steady, discernable progress. Asked if I still feel anger, lust, or other less-than-sterling emotions after my time in the meditative trenches, my answer is, "Definitely." However, I recover from them more rapidly than I once did. And yes, I still have bad habits to correct; I am no saint. But I hold to the concept of becoming one by not giving up, so I forge ahead with the tools I have been given.

What would be the point of writing this book or pursuing such matters unless becoming Self-realized is an attainable goal?

Since sexuality is such a large part of life and people's spiritual dance, sex merits distinct attention. I fully appreciate the senses but understand the nuances of sex and lust as a complex play between flesh and soul that mask primal yearnings for Spirit. I have come to value inner joy, purity, and selfless love above it. Without happiness, everything is empty, and happiness truly is a product of the inner Self, not sense experience. This is a tough lesson I keep revisiting, but we all have our crosses to bear, and I am no exception. On the mental plane, I am intellectual by nature but no longer feel constrained by intellectualism; I operate mostly by blending reason with intuition. Regarding the global stage, life dramas are no less important but are less angst inducing, and I see the world as an intricate laboratory with many lessons to learn and opportunities for refinement. I have faith in the divine process even though that faith can be challenged by mankind's ignorance. When all is said and done, I can vouch for what I have been taught and for how inner experience has shaped me. Crafting a spiritual life is a noble endeavor, and cultivating a relationship with Spirit—the fount of all good and happiness—is more enjoyable than anything else could be. The process takes time and is a long-term relationship, but what else in life produces so valuable an outcome? Happiness is one's true treasure. I am a happier person because of my practices. You can be, too. That alone is worth the effort.

Divine Union

Good endings are as gratifying as worthy beginnings. In closing this chapter and the body of this book, I want to emphasize that there is completion to the spiritual journey. It is the highest form of realization, the final homecoming gained by uniting one's soul with Spirit in creation and beyond. I have not experienced this state, so I can only describe it by borrowing from someone who has, Paramahansa Yogananda. In his poem "Samadhi," Yogananda conveys as literally as possible the epic majesty of God-consciousness. Here are a few excerpts from that poem to help convey the majesty of ultimate spiritual attainment:

> Vanished the veils of light and shade,
> Lifted every vapor of sorrow,
>
> . . . .
>
> Present past, future, no more for me,
> But ever-present, all-flowing I, I, everywhere.
>
> . . . .
>
> Thoughts of all men, past, present, to come,
> Every blade of grass, myself, mankind,
> Each particle of universal dust,
> Anger, greed, good, bad, salvation, lust,
> I swallowed, transmuted all.
>
> . . . .
>
> Thou art I, I am Thou,
> Knowing, Knower, Known, as One!
> Tranquilled, unbroken thrill, eternally living, ever-new peace.
> Enjoyable beyond imagination of expectancy, *samadhi* bliss!
>
> . . . .
>
> *Samadhi* but extends my conscious realm
> Beyond limits of the mortal frame
> To farthest boundary of eternity
> Where I, the Cosmic Sea,
> Watch the little ego floating in Me.
>
> . . . .
>
> From joy I came, for joy I live, in sacred joy I melt.
>
> . . . .
>
> I, in everything, enter the Great Myself.
>
> . . . .

A tiny bubble of laughter, I
Am become the Sea of Mirth Itself.[9]

Clearly, words cannot do justice to an experience that can only be known experientially and that transcends the limitations of mortal intellect. Suffice it to say that the ever-new consciousness, existence, and bliss of Spirit provide the eternal fulfillment we all seek, and does so in a manner that beggars description. This triumph of the Spirit is our birthright. Others have paved the way; now follow suit and reclaim your destiny.

13

Making the Commitment: Practice Guidelines

L ife is a school with vital lessons through which we eventually realize our essential Self. That is its purpose; all else is secondary. Approached with proper attitude, a marvelous adventure awaits. The journey becomes increasingly joyful and satisfying as methods for attaining soul insight are learned. A firm spiritual life is built by harnessing oneself to Spirit and living in harmony with cosmic laws. There may be bumps on the road, but through it all a harbor of calm insight serves to stabilize, guide, and inspire amid challenges of daily living. And while process is critical, the goal of divine union must never be lost. In the final analysis, it is what matters most.

This book has sought to provide invaluable skills to achieve these ends. Practice them to the best of your ability, and, while learning to swim in the sea of Spirit, help others learn to swim also. We are all in this together. From joy we came, in joy we must try to live, and in infinite joy we shall one day melt again.

GUIDELINES

After reviewing an earlier draft of this book, a friend said, "Tell me what my steps should be. Show me a road map." In response, I compiled seven steps augmenting the book's content with a how-to-proceed guide. A rationale for each step is given, yet I advise readers to personalize them to fit their own unique inclinations.

Step 1: Correct Attitude

Right attitude can be exercised anywhere, anytime. However, conscientiousness is the key. It is not enough just to practice meditation and prayer; anyone can do that. What makes spiritual practice alive is the ability to link inner work with correct attitude and action, moment to moment, day by day. This constant attention is also a foundation of mindfulness meditation practices that derive from Buddhist tradition. There is a saying that moments are more important than years, for if we can be happy, loving, and compassionate in the moment, then the years will take care of themselves. How we are now is the barometer for how we shall become later. Concentrate on maintaining correct attitude and behavior; then remain vigilant. That is the key to successful application of the ten qualities of self-control in thought and deed. If you wish, try focusing on one enhancing quality for a period, and then switch to another. Be creative in your attempts to improve. The important thing in transformation is making the consistent effort.

Step 2: Create a Sacred Space

Joseph Campbell referred to places used for spiritual practice as sacred spaces. This term is well suited to our purposes. As we now know, everything is energy. All actions create vibrations that also imbue areas of related activity with corresponding "vibrational signatures." For example, kitchens develop cooking vibrations, libraries those of study, and so forth. I suggest heeding this principle by fashioning your own sacred space, for it can impact spiritual practice significantly. Here are a few ways to do this:

Select a room or corner of a room for meditation. Choose a room, or part of one, and use it solely for spiritual practice. When entering this space, learn to immediately disengage the mind from all matters except the Divine. A vibrational field will gradually accumulate that is ideal for spiritual endeavors, and it gets richer over time. I have found my meditation space particularly nourishing when returning from travel or a stressful day; the uplifting atmosphere quickly aligns my consciousness to a higher state. To maintain the integrity of your space, educate household members not to conduct unrelated activities there or disturb you when you are "in session." My wife knows I will not talk about non-spiritual matters when in my meditation room, so if necessary, I step outside to do so. And, lest anyone accuse you of being selfish with your space and time, know that your efforts do benefit others. Just as it takes time to fix a large, nourishing meal, once it is prepared, that food can feed many.

Face east or north. East is optimal. At first blush, it may seem odd that facing a certain direction could impact spiritual practice. One could also say it is strange that planets or stars influence us. But they do. It is a fact that sunlight impacts the development of serotonin as well as vitamin D. The moon affects ocean tides and, in anecdotal cases, can alter human personality. Ask policemen or doctors if they notice changes in crime rates or patient behavior during a full moon. One reason for this effect is gravity. Body fluids influenced by lunar gravity affect our chemistry and, in turn, our mood. Similar dynamics are at play regarding directional alignment and meditation. Correspondingly, many traditional cultures ascribe definite traits to cardinal points. Among Native Americans, the Cherokee, Hopi, and Navajo share a sentiment that all good things come from the east. The relevant principle in yogic systems is that subtle forces flow from the east to foster enlightenment; those of the north promote liberation. Call it inner radar or conditioned thinking, but I have experienced that facing east versus other directions while meditating does feel right somehow. Of course, it is more important to meditate, regardless of direction, than to skip practice because you lack a compass.

Make an altar. Altars are associated with places of worship, as they suggest spiritual things. For us, they can be both practical and symbolic. Burning herbs like sage purifies an environment, while lighting incense invokes a sense of sanctity and ethereal sweetness. Candles suggest divine light, and saintly images can inspire noble thoughts. If you have photographs of spiritual masters, place them on your altar and

periodically gaze into their eyes. As mentioned earlier, this practice is a way to elevate consciousness through subtle affinity and magnetic exchange. I have most of these things on my altar, whereas a friend prefers displaying seashells and earth-based items. What to place on your altar is a matter of taste, as the goal is to engage the mind with reverence for the Sacred, not to get carried away with objects or their veneration.

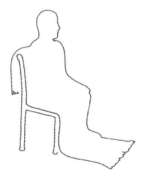

Sit on a woolen or silk cloth. Whether you sit on a chair or on a cushion, drape it with a woolen blanket, silk cloth, or both. If using a chair, place the material so that it runs over the seat back, under your buttocks, and onto the floor beneath your feet. If you are sitting on the ground, put down the cloth and then place a cushion atop it. Again, the reasons for doing so are magnetic. Earth-based currents pull energy downward, whereas we seek to lift energies up. Wool and silk insulate against these subtly adverse effects of earthly magnetism.

Step 3: Cultivating Environment

Environment derives from mental, emotional, and physical influences and must be constructed carefully. Yogananda stressed that environment is a stronger force than willpower due to its subtle influence. Spiritual aspirants should evaluate inner and outer influences to see if they reinforce higher goals and eliminate negative elements as necessary. By outer environment I mean friends, home, neighborhood, entertainment, reading material, and even clothes. All contribute to fashion a vibrational field that aids or hinders inner development. For instance, if you consistently wear drab clothes, associate with crooks, listen to rude music, or watch porn, these activities exert a negative influence. On the other hand, a combination of good friends, harmonious music, uplifting books, and healthy habits fosters wholesome refinement.

The same principles apply to one's inner environment of thought and attitude. These are most important from a spiritual perspective. Life conditions are significant, but thoughts, feelings, and related reactions produce maturity. Examine yourself in varied situations. Notice your response to people and situations. Are your thoughts primarily about God, service, and compassion or lust, anger, and greed? If you monitor this process, you will be impressed; the mind and heart are hard to govern. One could say that Jesus's mightiest miracle was his ability to return love for hate while being crucified. By doing so, he demonstrated mastery over human passions and the supremacy of divine love. When striving for excellence in your life, replace negative beliefs and behaviors with positive ones. In short, guard your mind and weed your thoughts, because they are the precursors of action.

Seek proactive, creative ways to remain uplifted and control environmental influences. For example, read inspiring books while on cardio machines at the health club, play chant CDs when driving about town, sneak in some meditation at lunch, and silently call to God all the time. Little things make a big difference in the trend of your thoughts and quality of life.

Step 4: Prayer

Pre-meditation prayers should be done with the love of God for the purpose of knowing God. They do not need to be fancy, just sincere. Invite Spirit to meditate with and through you, to guide and inspire the process of awakening. Then conclude meditation with a prayer of appreciation and blessing. Be aware of how fortunate you are even to contemplate the Divine. One of Yogananda's prayers I routinely use when closing a meditation is, "[Divine Mother/God/Spirit], may Thy love shine forever on the sanctuary of my devotion, and may I be able to awaken Thy love in all hearts."[1] Your approach may be unique; just make it heartfelt. Here is a story illustrating why genuine affection is always attractive:

My wife once invited various friends to drop by informally for my birthday. They were very kind and brought sundry cards, extended well wishes, and so forth. In the midst of this, two very young neighbor girls came in, grinning from ear to ear. They had not known about my birthday until five minutes earlier, yet, with huge smiles, handed me a sheet of paper with hand-drawn Xs and Os plus a colorful heart. It was an act of pure, spontaneous affection. Can you guess which of my cards I liked best?

Step 5: Practice Regularly

Many people wonder how long they should meditate and how often. Do what is joyful for as long as you can. A good start is to meditate fifteen to thirty minutes twice daily, first thing in the morning and before going to sleep. Gradually lengthen the sessions. As you develop "meditation muscles," try meditating for three hours straight once weekly, and periodically go for six hours. This length may seem overwhelming at first, but you will find long sessions very enjoyable as you get used to them and go deep. The most important thing is to set a daily practice time you can commit to and then do it. We are creatures of habit, so make the habit and then let it make you.

Along with regular practice, be mindful of the following two points. First, be considerate of others. Life requires balance. Be fair to those who share your house and life by meditating when you will not compromise their needs. My schedule is designed to meet certain classical standards plus avoid interfering with my wife's activities. Inner growth is a priority but should not be used to avoid work or life responsibilities. All legitimate duties may be seen as assigned by God and must be fulfilled to live in a respectful and balanced manner.

Second, monitor the body. Relaxation and correct posture are vital for meditation. When sitting in a chair or on a cushion, position yourself so the hips are higher than the knees. This keeps the spine straight and body musculature at ease. Next, drop the body—relax and forget about it entirely—and then dive deep within.

Step 6: Practice Model

Here is a basic routine outline. If you wish to meditate longer than presented, do so.

Pre-Meditation Activity

Energizing Exercises—five to ten minutes

Stretching—five to ten minutes

Meditation Session

Breath/Energy-Balancing Exercises

Invocation Prayer

Concentration Technique—ten minutes

Inner Sound Technique—ten minutes

Period of Stillness—ten minutes

Receive and Expand

Pray

Receive and Expand

Closing Prayer

Following Your Practice

- Hold on to the aftereffects of meditation for as long as possible.

- Apply that feeling to all activities and with all people.

- Silently keep communion with and call to Spirit constantly.

These tips might seem like pleasant afterthoughts, but they are extremely potent directions to help spiritualize your life. People tend to think spiritual practice is just about doing certain things or cultivating particular states of mind. While partially true, the hidden element is holding on to the aftereffects of one's practice for as long as possible. By doing this we gradually infuse all activities with a spiritual perspective and transform ourselves, as well as our lives, accordingly.

Step 7: Commit and Enjoy

As oft repeated, the journey of awakening is not a contest to be won by strained effort. Do not judge yourself or strain for results. Do your best. Commit to a long-term relationship with Spirit, and be dedicated, loyal, and persistent. This process is not a gamble; it will pay off, and with the highest returns, if you do your part properly. Nothing separates us from Spirit other than the illusion of separation.

Now is the time to rend this illusion and resurrect your Self in divine glory.

A CLOSING WORD

Thank you, reader, for giving this book your time and attention. Considering the harried pace of modern living, the financial worries, family issues, and global concerns, there are many other ways you could have spent your time. Nonetheless, the pursuit of Spirit through meditation and the spiritual life is of greatest value. Nothing can be achieved in this world—no rifts mended, diseases cured, wars abolished, policies changed, or environments healed—without the life, intelligence, love, compassion, wisdom, and truth given us by God. Developing a spiritual life is not a selfish endeavor, but the highest form of service. Through meditation we refine ourselves, and as divine light and love increasingly pervade our thoughts and deeds, we become agents of change for those in our immediate circle plus society at large. The effects ripple out in subtle but real ways that influence and uplift all. As you pursue the spiritual life, know that you do make a difference. On behalf of others and myself I say, "Bravo!"

Finally, and most importantly, regardless of what you have done in life or how unworthy you feel, divine love is unconditional and eternal.

You are of the Infinite. Hide no longer; tarry no more. Spirit yearns for your love and is thrilled whenever you, his/her child, wish to return Home.

Appendix:
Spirituality and Religion

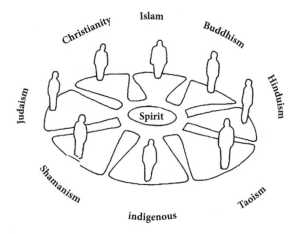

WHAT IS SPIRITUALITY?

Spirituality is an increasingly popular topic and is addressed by innumerable books, magazines, research studies, television shows, and movies. Embraced by many as an alternative to religion, it elicits mixed responses. Some see spirituality as a progressive reform movement that strips away doctrine and dogma to reveal the primary elements around which most religious movements have been historically formed. Others may view it as something misguided and potentially corrosive to enduring theologies. Consequently, as spirituality emerges, it is often met with both enthusiasm and resistance. I maintain that spirituality exists at the core of every religion yet is often hidden behind veils that require discernment to see past. This appendix discusses both spirituality and religion while refraining from dissecting their every nuance. Given the subjective nature of these topics, clarification is necessary to form a foundation upon which to build, but it is a matter that could form a book unto itself. Since the subject is important and relevant, I address it, but do so as an appendix because the ideas and terminology discussed may seem dry or academic. If such is the case, feel free to skip this and know that you have been well served by the content already presented.

Spirituality is not nebulous. It is an enlightening process that comes from understanding core components of existence. Like a sophisticated construction schematic, it depicts reality as it is and addresses life in relationship to a higher consciousness paradigm of immutable divine principles that transcend ideological differences. Every faith deals with essential spiritual elements while calling them by varied names or viewing them in unique ways. That these essentials are addressed in so many different ways does not negate their existence or the necessity to live in alignment with them. For example, every major religious tradition posits an ultimate goal, termed *enlightenment*, *samadhi*, or *heaven*. Each shares common moral codes or concepts of sanctity that culminate in supreme attainment. Each holds that creation exists and functions lawfully and that a noncorporeal element of consciousness, soul, abides within the body. These principles are as fundamental to spirituality as addition and subtraction are to math. They remain constant and fixed to diverse linguistic or cultural contexts. Spirituality, then, is the effort to discover and live in harmony with universal laws without obstructionist ideologies that might otherwise obscure their realization.

This next series of views offers perspectives on spirituality paired with opportunity for commentary.

Perspective 1

Random House Webster's College Dictionary describes spirituality as "the quality or fact of being spiritual." Of *spiritual* it says: "of or pertaining to a) the soul or spirit as distinguished from the physical nature; b) the spirit as the seat of the moral or religious nature; c) sacred things or matters; religious."[1]

Commentary

The first part of the definition suggests that soul or spirit is distinct from the physical body. This is only partially true. More accurately, soul consciousness and life energy emanate from Spirit as light does from the sun. These intelligent elements fashion three increasingly dense subtle bodies that cumulatively manifest in physical form. What we see as a physical body is actually an integrated system of soul, life force, and consciousness commingling, coalescing, and coexisting on a material plane. At the time of death the soul and subtle bodies depart the physical frame, leaving the body an uninhabited husk, while they abide on more subtle planes of existence.

Parts b and c above do not differ from what I said earlier: spirituality is the essence of sacred matters and will be elaborated upon shortly.

Perspective 2

In "Reflections on Human Spirituality for the Worksite," Brian Seaward defines spirituality as "a maturation process of higher consciousness with respect to an insightful and nurturing relationship with oneself and others, the development of a strong value system and the cultivation of a meaningful purpose in life."[2]

Commentary

Seaward emphasizes the development of values, behaviors, and relationships that give meaning to life and enhance the act of living. While sociologically prudent, his definition remains a bit vague because it lacks affiliation to a substantive metaphysical paradigm. His use of the term *maturation*, however, is compelling, for it implies an evolutionary process that promotes individual or collective development. This allusion to an elevating power may have been unintentional, but it does link contextually to a higher-power framework. If not for the ability to progress, especially in the realm of consciousness, we would be trapped in a limiting quagmire of mental stasis. Fortunately, there is a mysterious force that propels us from lower strata of awareness to increasingly refined expressions of human potential. Within that spectrum we witness a range of personas from brutish to saintly. Less-evolved individuals demonstrate self-absorbed, survivalist, and procreative traits not unlike the animal kingdom. Their world is constrictive and limited primarily to themselves. Saints exhibit a diminishment of ego that allows them to perceive the Sacred in all. Sensing all life as derived from a common source, they compassionately embrace existence in all its myriad aspects as a manifestation of their unified, macrocosmic Self.

Perspective 3

The Spirituality in Healthcare Committee of the Mayo Clinic defined spirituality as "a process by which one discovers inner wisdom and vitality that gives meaning and purpose to all life events."[3]

Commentary

This definition has merit but uses terms without explaining them sufficiently, an oversight that compromises understanding. For example, what is wisdom? What is vitality? What is inner? I describe wisdom as understanding truth and acting in harmony with it; vitality as abundant, intrinsic life force that flows unhindered and can be augmented by right use of will; and inner refers to the soul domain, those subtle embodiments of Spirit that abide within physical form. These elements must be allied to sacred cosmology or they will lack meaningful orientation.

Perspective 4

This last definition of spirituality is mine and is, I believe, the most comprehensive. "Spirituality is the essence of all faith traditions, the immutable Truth hiding behind and within every religious form. It is the medium through which persons establish direct communion, and union, with Spirit regardless of formal orientation. Spirituality is both the immediate experience of That-Which-Is-Holy, the Higher Power by whatever name, and living by the relevant principles, precepts, and practices that foster this relationship and the fruits of its attainment."[4]

These points are essential to understanding spirituality:

- Spirituality is not religiosity.

- Spirituality is a way of life attuned to cosmic laws, not relative beliefs.

- Spirituality holds that each soul can have, and is entitled to, direct experience of Spirit.

- Spirituality views the nature of soul and its purpose for earthly incarnation as universal.

- Spirituality is intrinsically sacred and moral. One cannot practice it correctly and be profane.

- Spiritual realization requires right methods, plus devotion, to be optimally effective.

- Spirituality includes both an impersonal and a personal divine aspect.

- The impersonal aspect is mathematically precise and aloof cosmic law. The personal aspect is the cosmic intelligence/love/wisdom force that can incarnate in innumerable forms to demonstrate divine teachings and qualities.

WHAT IS RELIGION AND HOW IS IT DIFFERENT FROM SPIRITUALITY?

Perspective 1

Random House Webster's College Dictionary defines religion as "a) . . . a set of beliefs concerning the cause, nature, and purpose of the universe, especially when considered as the creation of a superhuman agency or agencies, usually involving devotional and ritual observances, and often containing a moral code for the conduct of human affairs. . . . ; b) . . . a specific fundamental set of beliefs and practices generally agreed upon by a number of persons or sects."[5]

Commentary

These definitions represent religion as popular origin-theory concepts, socioethical guidelines, ritual, and consensual thinking, not definitive insight. Not to discredit collective beliefs, but they are not intrinsically factual. Intuitive experience offers spiritual substance, while intellect and opinion offer conjecture. Science tests theories to ascertain validity. If discredited, they are rejected; if proven, they become law. These standards should also apply to religion, metaphysics, or anything that impacts life choices and quality. Shoppers seek facts about commercial items. Why should spiritual or religious matters differ? The principal reason is that people often see religion as beyond their ability to scrutinize. This mindset, often crafted by those who enjoy domination over others, fosters blind obeisance to clerical authority rather than license to individual realization and understanding. Genuine mystical revelation has nothing to do with position or power but stems from direct perception. "I thank thee, O Father, Lord of heaven and earth, because thou hast hid these things from the wise and prudent, and hast revealed them unto babes."[6]

Many religions remain hamstrung by constricting dogma, ritual, and the need to retain control. Such rigidity has prompted numerous truth seekers to reach beyond their original faith paths to more expansive, esoterically informative, and less hierarchal paradigms. The cause of this exodus stems from a natural soul craving, the desire for intimate acquaintance with the Sacred. Unfortunately, most Abrahamic traditions have historically not nourished experientially rooted inner practices but, instead, have taught that prayer, scripture, or grace alone suffices. Restricted mystical access has contributed to a crisis of connection that has prompted the increased acceptance of meditation over time. Meditation produces unfiltered communion with the holy and is the most substantive means by which scripture, doctrine, or dogma can be evaluated. This capacity to apprehend divine truth directly, as well as the desire to do so, is a hallmark of spiritual practice but is not of usual concern for most religionists. To the latter, such pursuits may seem inappropriate, even hubristic. Meditative insight, however, provides realizations that can corroborate accepted theological tenets or challenge them. Accordingly, Jesus spoke authoritatively about spiritual matters because of his divine perception, not doctrinal fidelity: "Verily, verily, I say unto thee, We speak that we do know, and testify that we have seen."[7] This important concept is echoed by these notable quotes:

> Whoever theorizes his religion offends
> against the Way of God, and peace. Heretic!
> . . . .
> All this learned talk is ignorance.
> Station and state discard it.[8]

As a matter of psychological fact, mystical states of a well-pronounced and emphatic sort are usually authoritative over those who have them. They have been "there," and know. It is vain for rationalism to grumble about this. . . . Our own more "rational" beliefs are based on evidence exactly similar in nature to that which mystics quote for theirs. Our senses, namely, have assured us of certain states of fact; but mystical experiences are as direct perceptions of fact for those who have them as any sensations ever were for us. . . . The mystic is, in short, invulnerable, and must be left, whether we relish it or not, in undisturbed enjoyment of his creed.[9]

Interestingly, religion arises almost exclusively from seminal sacred events and related inspirations. Sadly, mystical realizations typically become codified, institutionalized dogmas that inhibit rather than vivify efforts toward personal illumination. In short, religion disseminates mythic theology whenever it fails to foster, or opposes outright, intuitively gleaned perception of higher realities. Truth is not a matter of consensus, and, regardless of how many agree with an idea, accord is not the same as accuracy.

Perspective 2

The Mayo Clinic Spirituality in Healthcare Committee defines religion as "a formalized system of beliefs and practices shared by a group."[10]

Commentary

This description could as easily apply to college fraternities as to worshipful institutions, since it fails to identify what beliefs or practices people share and why and how such systems become formalized. People can believe anything and frequently do; loyalty to ideas—no matter how fervent—does not guarantee veracity. For instance, fundamentalists of any path who cling to doctrine or dogma effectively worship at altars of ignorance because they champion rote conduct over intuitive discernment. This behavior perpetuates an unquestioning ideology and, in all likelihood, obscures truth.

Thorough understanding should be the basis for theological fidelity, not consensual agreement. A fine example of this is depicted in the yoga sutras, particularly the eightfold path of Patanjali. His first two steps include ten guidelines for right behavior, much like the Ten Commandments.

These guidelines are not random, socially prudent dictums. They are distillates of proper conduct fashioned from awareness of our essential unity with Spirit. Perfecting each "rule" results in the manifestation of a divine attribute, like a flower that blossoms when mature, and testifies to the fruit, or causative effect, of living in flawless harmony with spiritual precepts. Again, religious tenets lean toward unquestioning compliance, while spiritual practices lean toward transparency and clear metaphysical understanding. Yogananda's spiritual master, Sri Yukteswar, expressed this latter sentiment perfectly when he said, "Many teachers will tell you to believe; then they put out your eyes of reason and instruct you to follow only their logic. But I want you to keep your eyes of reason open; in addition, I will open in you another eye, the eye of wisdom."[11]

Perspective 3

My definition of religion is "the organization and measured enactment of spiritually based rules, rituals, and doctrine surrounding and developing from the life and teachings of a Founding Individual or Revelatory Source."[12]

Commentary

The key words here are *organization* and *spiritually based.* Only very unique souls have initiated world religions. Their teachings, inspired by revelation, issued from a source of truth to fit the needs and customs of the time. The passing of their spiritual legacies undoubtedly fell to less advanced, but well-meaning, persons who recorded sermons and deeds yet lacked the fire of original inspiration and understanding. Seeking to preserve authenticity, such stewards inevitably arranged dispensations into manageable doctrines and, intentionally or not, supplanted the verities that spawned them. These doctrines become fixed into established, venerated forms, and dogma rules the day.

These comments are not aimed at those who embrace their faith and apply its tenets in pluralistic, loving, and humble ways. Indeed, such practices are spiritually minded and offer great value: pursuit of God, holy standards, and the motivation to apply them. Widespread dissatisfaction with religious institutions has arisen in modern times, however, because of the historic perpetuation of exclusivist practices or ideas that control people or cause significant suffering through bigotry and hateful misconduct. For example, the First Council of Nicaea, AD 325, co-opted early Christian doctrine to fashion an ideological consensus, a hierarchical governing structure, and a theological distribution system that contrasted significantly with certain views shared by other original Christians, the Gnostic community in particular. What is more, there is significant scholarly controversy about the authenticity of written material in the New Testament; texts or writ ascribed to certain apostles or authors may very well not have been written by them at all. I cannot fully develop these matters here, but suffice it to say that the issues and teachings involved are so significant that the common Christian canon may differ quite radically from what Jesus actually taught. Mutation of creeds occurs in all religions when wisdom is altered by ignorance, political expediency, or convenience. Despite this tendency to distort truth, the craving for it impels the human heart and soul past fallacy and stasis. When Jesus asked Saint Francis to "rebuild my church," he did not mean a literal reconstruction project—something Francis initially misinterpreted—but rather, he wanted the essential spiritual basis of his teachings reanimated. That need to live a life of personal communion with Spirit still exists and is why many religious institutions are increasingly offering their brand of meditative practices for interested parishioners: It provides soul nourishment of a direct and inner kind.

There are three key differences between spirituality and religion:

Spirituality is universal. Spirituality is inherently universal and pluralistic. Truth is considered immutable yet variously manifest. It embraces multiplicity as a natural, creative expression of the One. Religions tend to be exclusive, not due to original teachings so much as to the corrosive impact of ignorance over time. Even religious inclusivism retains an arrogant stance of having the one true path. And, clearly, fundamentalism of any sort limits ideological options. Those who walk a definite religious path yet validate other traditions may be said to practice their religion spiritually, i.e., with expansive tolerance.

Spirituality advocates personal access to the Divine. Spirituality advocates direct experience of the Sacred and supports each soul's right to attain divine union regardless of faith orientation. Religions, on the other hand, often relegate such access to hierarchical authority figures, thereby perpetuating dependency patterns and inhibiting personal realization of God.

Spirituality values law over doctrine. The essence of spiritual practice involves understanding and applying cosmic laws that govern universal operations, i.e., truth. While paths to Spirit may differ, the principles involved do not. For example, there is not Christian gravity versus Muslim, Jewish, or Buddhist gravity; there is only the law of gravity. Questionable dogmas or interpretations about spiritual doctrines can be readily bypassed by adhering to common cosmic law.

Comparing religion to spirituality may seem antagonistic, but it helps clarify what each represents. Both strive to foster soul growth and are not mutually exclusive. Religion must contain the elements of spirituality to be effective, and spirituality must honor the framework of organized religion as a vehicle for implementation. It is the nature of spirituality to be pure; it is the nature of religion to attempt to carry forth this purity. When religious teachings align with divine law they are authentic, hence, spiritual. Whenever religious tenets stray, spirituality exists to bring them back to eternal truth.

The Inner Life

Like siblings, spirituality and religion share common parentage, a concept called the inner life. The inner life is the essence of spirituality and the basis for all genuine religious activity. It comes from the fact that every religion has two sets of teachings: outer doctrine (dogmatic and ritual-istic) and inner tradition (mystical or spiritual), both of which exist simultaneously. To clarify the distinctions, consider the analogy of a wal-nut. Outer, or exoteric, teachings are like a walnut's shell. Its hardness is ideal for protective purposes and withstands the rigors of time to guard prized contents. This shell satisfies those for whom surface teachings and general concepts about God are acceptable. Others of keener spiritual appetite find such fare lacking and want to crack the shell for more sus-taining nourishment, its inner meat—mystical, esoteric teachings that foster spiritual insight and realization.

Yet how exactly does "inner" differ from "outer"? The inner life is based on direct experience, a point so vital that I emphasize it repeatedly. Looking at a photo of fire is not the same as feeling its heat. Likewise, knowing Spirit by personal realization is far different from reading or hearing about it secondhand. The preeminent Christian scholar St. Thomas Aquinas understood this distinction very well. He had such a profound mystical experience while celebrating Mass on December 6, 1273, that afterward he stopped writing his great work, the *Summa Theologica*. Asked why he had discontinued, Aquinas replied, "I cannot go on. . . . All that I have written seems to me like so much straw com-pared to what I have seen and what has been revealed to me."[13] A similar example of inner-versus-outer knowing took place in the life of the not-able spiritual master Sri Ramakrishna. During his "debate" with a renowned religious scholar the latter gave a scriptural lecture that had the audience cheering approval. Sri Ramakrishna was conventionally uneducated, so when he took the stage he simply began repeating Ma, a term for God as the Divine Mother. With each repetition he went deeper inside until he entered a state of spiritual ecstasy. Ramakrishna demon-strated divine realization—he grasped those matters directly—but the scholar could only discuss them theoretically.

The inner life is not the academic life. It strives to uplift soul awareness above ego identification and to induce recollection of its divine origin in Spirit. It focuses on soul qualities so that knowledge of Spirit may be revealed when the worshiper and worshiped reunite in a holy bond. This state is hard for average persons to understand, as their awareness is ordinarily identified with the world. The very concept that fulfillment can be had by loving God or by spending time nurturing a divine relationship is difficult for such persons to grasp. The reality hidden from them is that Spirit is joy itself and the soul, being a part of God, has kindred attributes. Happiness seems externally acquired when shrouded by egoistic delusion. Those steeped in soul consciousness know differently; unalloyed joy can be had without sensory dependence. Although a certain amount of discipline is necessary to cultivate the inner life, once achieved, it clearly is not perceived as a deprived condition. Rather, it leads one from misleading addiction to transient sense pleasures to sustained gratification in Spirit. This does not mean material things cannot be appreciated, merely that we should not become attached to them. Enduring fulfillment can be had only by uniting with the source of fulfillment, God. Jesus expounded on this truth in the parable of the Samarian woman: "Whosoever drinketh of this water [material life] shall thirst again: But whosoever drinketh of the water that I shall give him [spiritual ecstasy] shall never thirst [desires forever satisfied]; but the water that I shall give him shall be in him a well of water springing up into everlasting life [eternal union with God]."[14]

The mystical poets Jelaluddin Rumi and Omar Khayyam similarly praise the inner life and its liberating consequences. Here are two expressions of their insights, Rumi's first, then Khayyam:

We Three

My love wanders the rooms, melodious,
flute notes, plucked wires,
full of a wine the Magi drank
on the way to Bethlehem.
We are three.

The moon comes
from its quiet corner, puts a pitcher of water

down in the center. The circle
of surface flames.
One of us kneels to kiss the threshold.
One drinks, with wine-flames playing over his face.
One watches the gathering,
and says to any cold onlookers,
This dance is the joy of existence.
I am filled with you.

Skin, blood, bone, brain, and soul.
There's no room for lack of trust, or trust.
Nothing in this existence but That existence.[15]

The Rubaiyat, Quatrain 74 (poem title)

Ah, Moon of my Delight, who know'st no wane,
The Moon of Heav'n is rising once again:
How oft hereafter rising shall she look
Through this same Garden after me—in vain![16]

In an interpretation of the Rubaiyat, *Wine of the Mystic,* Yogananda described the "Moon of my Delight" as God and the "Moon of Heav'n" as the cosmos.[17] Khayyam was said to have attained spiritual liberation from compulsory reincarnation, hence the "Garden"—nature—could hold sway over him no longer. Heeding the soul's yearning to return home, Khayyam was freed in Spirit forever. Such is the goal of the inner life and the purpose of spiritual practice. Whereas intellect approaches Spirit theoretically, the inner life fosters direct experience of the Sacred. Such discernment produces wisdom which, when combined with meditation-born insights, yields divine realization and, ultimately, freedom.

Notes

Preface

1. Paramahansa Yogananda, *Self-Realization Fellowship Lessons*, S-2 P-52/1 (Los Angeles: Self-Realization Fellowship, 1984), 2.

Chapter 1

1. Walter Hill and Alan Geoffrion, *Broken Trail*, Part 1 (New York: AMC, 2006).
2. Pierre Teilhard de Chardin, *The Phenomenon of Man*, trans. Bernard Wall (New York: Harper & Brothers, 1959).
3. 1 John 2:15–17 (KJV).
4. Bhagavad Gita 12.18–25, trans. Edwin Arnold, www.sacred-texts.com/hin/gita/bg12.htm, www.sacred-texts.com, www.sacred-texts.com/hin/gita/index.htm.
5. Luke 11:9 (KJV).
6. First set forth in *Philosophiae Naturalis Principia Mathematica* (Mathematical Principles of Natural Philosophy), 1687.

Chapter 2

1. Rev. 1:8 (KJV).
2. Bhagavad Gita 10.34, 9.7, in David White, trans., *The Bhagavad Gita: A New Translation with Commentary* (New York: Peter Lang Publishing, 1989), 141, 123.
3. Paramahansa Yogananda, *Self-Realization Fellowship Lessons*, S-1 P-11 (see preface, n. 1), 5.
4. Paramahansa Yogananda, "Quickening Human Evolution," *East West Magazine*, January–February 1929, 5.
5. Paramahansa Yogananda, *Where There Is Light* (Los Angeles: Self-Realization Fellowship, 1988), 5–6.
6. Ramana Maharshi, *Talks With Sri Ramana Maharshi*, Talk 3 (Tamil Nadu, South India: V. S. Ramanan, 2000), 3.

NOTES

7. John 8:32 (KJV).
8. Paramahansa Yogananda, *Autobiography of a Yogi*, 13th ed., 13th paperback printing (Los Angeles: Self-Realization Fellowship, 1999), 319–20.
9. First set forth in René Descartes, *Principia Philosophiae* (Principles of Philosophy, 1644), part 1, article 7.
10. Gen. 2:16–17 (NKJV).
11. Rev. 3:12 (KJV).
12. St. Theresa of Avila, *The Way of Perfection* (New York: Doubleday, 1964), chap. 21.
13. St. Theresa of Avila, Poem IX, in *Complete Works St. Teresa of Avila*, vol. 3 (London: Sheed & Ward, 1963), 288.
14. Bhagavad Gita 4.7–8, in Paramahansa Yogananda, *God Talks With Arjuna: The Bhagavad Gita*, vol. 1 (Los Angeles: Self-Realization Fellowship, 1995), 439.

Chapter 3

1. John 6:44 (KJV).
2. Matthew 3:15 (KJV).
3. Matthew 9:14–15 (KJV).
4. John 1:12 (KJV).
5. Swami Chetanananda, *God Lived with Them: Life Stories of Sixteen Monastic Disciples of Sri Ramakrishna* (St. Louis: Vedanta Society of St. Louis, 1997), 29.
6. Christopher Isherwood, *Ramakrishna and His Disciples* (Hollywood, CA: Vedanta Press, 1965), 197.
7. Paramahansa Yogananda, *Man's Eternal Quest* (Los Angeles: Self-Realization Fellowship, 1975), 114.
8. Paramahansa Yogananda, *Autobiography of a Yogi*, 141 (see chap. 2, n. 8).

Chapter 4

1. Paramahansa Yogananda, *Autobiography of a Yogi*, 287 (see chap. 2, n. 8).

Chapter 5

1. John 10:34 (KJV).
2. Isaiah 45:5, 7 (KJV).
3. *Random House Webster's College Dictionary*, 1992, s.v. "universe."

4. Colossians 1:16 (KJV).
5. Bhagavad Gita 7.6–7, in Paramahansa Yogananda, *God Talks With Arjuna: The Bhagavad Gita*, vol. 2 (Los Angeles: Self-Realization Fellowship, 1995), 674–75.
6. "Chief Seattle's 1854 Oration," quoted in column by Henry A. Smith, *Seattle Sunday Star*, Oct. 29, 1887, http://www.halcyon.com/arborhts/chiefsea.html.
7. John Muir, *My First Summer in the Sierra* (Boston: Houghton Miflin, 1911), 110, Sierra Club, The John Muir Exhibit, http://www.sierraclub.org/john_muir_exhibit/writings.
8. Bhagavad Gita 12.5, in Paramahansa Yogananda, *God Talks With Arjuna*, vol. 2, 842.
9. Bhagavad Gita 18.46, ibid., 1063.
10. Gal. 6:7 (KJV).
11. Bhagavad Gita 9.34, *God Talks With Arjuna*, vol. 2, 766.
12. Matthew 26:42 (KJV).
13. John 1:12 (KJV).
14. Lev. 20:7–8 (KJV).
15. Matthew 22.37 (KJV).
16. Bhagavad Gita 12.8, in Paramahansa Yogananda, *God Talks With Arjuna*, vol. 2, 845.
17. Buddha's Vow for Enlightenment, in Paramahansa Yogananda, *Whispers From Eternity* (Los Angeles: Self-Realization Publishing House, 1949), 55.
18. Luke 8:43–48 (KJV).
19. Paramahansa Yogananda, "The Philosopher's Stone," in the *Praecepta Lessons* (Los Angeles: Self-Realization Fellowship, 1935).
20. Exod. 20:2–4 (KJV).
21. Bhagavad Gita 7.21, in Paramahansa Yogananda, *God Talks With Arjuna*, vol. 2, 696.
22. Lao Tzu, *Tao Te Ching*, trans. Ch'u Ta-Kao (London: George Allen & Unwin, 1959), 1.
23. John 1:1 (KJV).
24. Paramahansa Yogananda, "Wisdom: 'A Para-Gram'" (Los Angeles: Self-Realization Fellowship, 1984), 39.
25. St. Augustine, *Confessions*, I, 1, "Saint Augustine of Hippo," *the WORD among us*, http://wau.org/resources/article/saint_augustine_of_hippo_354_430/.
26. Phil. 4:7 (KJV).
27. Paramahansa Yogananda, *Autobiography of a Yogi*, 172 (see ch. 2, n. 8).
28. Bhagavad Gita 7.14, in Paramahansa Yogananda, *God Talks With Arjuna*, vol. 2, 685.

NOTES

Chapter 6

1. Patanjali, *Yoga Sutras*, trans. Sri Swami Satchidananda, http://www.athayoganusasanam.com/?zone=browse_sutras&pada. All section epigraphs from Patanjali in this and the next chapter are from this source unless otherwise noted.
2. M. K. Gandhi, *The Gospel of Nonviolence (Harijan)* (Ahmedabad, India: Navjeevan Trust, 1936), 236.
3. Martin Luther King, Jr., "The Meaning of Non-Violence," http://www.mkgandhi.org/nonviolence/philosophy.htm.
4. Matt. 5.43–46 (NKJV).
5. *Yoga Sutras of Patanjali*, trans. Swami Jnaneshvara Bharati, 30, http://www.swamij.com/pdf/yogasutrasinterpretive.pdf.
6. M. K. Gandhi, *All Men Are Brothers* (Paris: UNESCO, 1969), 65, http://unesdoc.unesco.org/images/0007/000710/071082eo.pdf.
7. "Ghandi's Views on God," *Mahatma Gandhi Information Website*, http://www.gandhi-manibhavan.org/gandhiphilosophy/philosophy_god_god.htm.
8. Isa. 55:8 (KJV).
9. Matt. 16:23 (KJV).
10. Marianne Williamson, *A Return to Love: Reflections on the Principles of a Course in Miracles* (New York: HarperCollins, 1992), 190.
11. John 5:30 (KJV).
12. Bhagavad Gita 9.18, in Paramahansa Yogananda, *God Speaks with Arjuna*, vol. 2, 758 (see chap. 5, n. 5).
13. Paramahansa Yogananda, *Autobiography of a Yogi*, 133–34 (see chap. 2, n. 8).
14. Bhagavad Gita 12.11, *The Bhagavad Gita*, ed. Ramanda Prasad (Fremont, CA: The American Gita Society, 1995), 197.
15. John 4:13–14 (KJV).
16. Matt. 6:21 (KJV).
17. J. W. McCrindle, *Ancient India as Described by Megasthenes and Arrian* (London: Trubner & Co., 1877), http://bharatabharati.wordpress.com/2009/10/04/alexanders-encounter-with-dandamis-at-taxila/.

Chapter 7

1. Bhagavad Gita 9.26, "Bhaktivedanta VedaBase: Bhagavad-gītā As It Is," http://vedabase.net/bg/9/26/en3.
2. Mark 12:43–44 (KJV).

3. Bhagavad Gita 12.10, Paramahansa Yogananda, *God Talks with Arjuna*, vol. 2, 846 (see chap. 5, n. 5).

4. Bhagavad Gita 6.30, ibid., 634.

5. *The Yoga Sutras of Patanjali: The Thread of Union*, 2:44, trans. BonGiovanni, http://www.sacred-texts.com/hin/yogasutr.htm.

6. Audrey Yoshiko Seo and Stephen Addis, *The Sound of One Hand: Paintings and Calligraphy by Zen Master Hakuin* (Boston: Shambhala, 2010).

7. Brother Angelo, "Saint Francis and Brother Ass," *franciscan,* January 1996, http://www.franciscanarchive.org.uk/1996jan-angelossf.html.

8. Pategama Gnanarama, *Essentials of Buddhism* (Singapore: Buddha Dharma Education Association, 2000), 25.

9. Wanda Mallette, Bob Morrison, and Patti Ryan, "Lookin' for Love," 1980.

10. Matt. 15:11 (KJV).

11. Matt. 6:25 (KJV).

12. Matt. 5:8 (KJV).

13. Rev. 3:21 (KJV).

14. William Shakespeare, *King Lear*, Act 1, Scene 1 (New Haven, CT: Yale University Press, 2007), 4.

15. Lao Tzu, *Tao Te Ching*, trans. James Legge, chap. 33, http://classics.mit.edu/Lao/taote.1.1.html.

16. Paramahansa Yogananda, *Autobiography of a Yogi*, 157, 165 (see chap. 2, n. 8).

Chapter 8

1. Bhagavad Gita 4.7, from *Rays of the One Light*, trans. Swami Kriyananda (Nevada City: CA, Crystal Clarity Publishers, 1996), 21.

2. John 3:17 (KJV).

3. Phil. 4:8 (KJV).

4. Randy Dotinga, "Subliminal Smiles Can Sway You," *HealthDay News*, May 27, 2005.

Chapter 9

1. Paramahansa Yogananda, *Self-Realization Fellowship Lessons*, S-1 P-6, 3 (see preface, n. 1).

2. St. Theresa of Avila, *The Interior Castle*, translation and introduction by Mirabai Starr, (New York: Berkley Publishing Group, 2003), 93.

3. John 3:14 (KJV).

4. Rev. 3:21 (KJV).
5. John 1:12 (KJV).
6. Swami Sri Yukteswar, *The Holy Science* (Los Angeles: Self-Realization Fellowship, 1984), 60.
7. James 1:22 (KJV).

Chapter 10

1. Luke 17:20–21 (KJV).
2. Bhagavad Gita 7.3. from *Rays of the One Light*, 53 (see chap. 8, n. 1).
3. Matt. 9:37 (KJV).
4. *Confessions of St. Augustine*, trans J. G. Pilkington (New York: Liveright Publishing Corp., 1943), bk. 7, chap. 7, 176.
5. Paramahansa Yogananda, *Autobiography of a Yogi*, 138 (see chap 2., n. 8).

Chapter 11

1. Matt. 4:4 (KJV).
2. Paramahansa Yogananda, *Autobiography of a Yogi*, 460 (see chap. 2, n. 8).
3. Mark 11:24 (KJV).
4. Matt. 6:6 (KJV).

Chapter 12

1. Rev. 3:12 (KJV).
2. Quoted in Dick de Ruiter, *Yoga & Sound* (Havelte, Holland: Binkey Kok Publications, 2005), 4, http://www.maisondesmiracles.nl/pdf/YOGA&SOUND_English.pdf.
3. Ibid.
4. Lao Tzu, *The Way of Life*, trans. R. B. Blakney (New York: New American Library, 1955), 25; and Charles H. Mackintosh, *Tao* (Wheaton, IL: Theosophical Publishing House, 1926), chaps. 83 and 84.
5. Paramahansa Yogananda, *Self-Realization Fellowship Lessons*, S-2 P-28 (see preface, n. 1), 2.
6. Zech. 4:2–3 (KJV).
7. Ezek. 28:14 (KJV).
8. Rev. 1:10, 12 (KJV).
9. Paramahansa Yogananda, *Whisper From Eternity*, 191–94 (see chap. 5, n. 17).

Chapter 13

1. Paramahansa Yogananda, *Autobiography of a Yogi*, 287 (see chap. 2, n. 8).

Appendix

1. *Random House Webster's College Dictionary*, 1992, s.v. "spirituality."
2. B. L. Seaward, "Reflections on Human Spirituality for the Worksite," *American Journal of Health Promotion*, 9, no. 2 Jan./Feb. 1995: 165–68.
3. Richard Leider, *The Power of Purpose: Find Meaning, Live Longer, Better* (San Francisco: Berrett-Koehler Publishers, 2010), 131.
4. Alan L. Pritz, *Pocket Guide To Meditation* (Berkeley, CA: The Crossing Press, 1997), 13.
5. *Random House Webster's College Dictionary*, 1992, s.v. "religion."
6. Matt. 11:25 (KJV).
7. John 3:11 (KJV).
8. Muhyiddin Ibn El-Arabi, *What the Seeker Needs: Essays on Spiritual Practice, Oneness, Majesty and Beauty* (New York: Threshold Books, 1992), 15.
9. William James, from *The Varieties of Religious Experience*, quoted in *The Philosophy of Learning* (Belmont, CA: Thomson Wadsworth, 2003), 107.
10. Alan L. Pritz, "Spirituality in the Workplace," in Liz Winfield, *A Trainer's Guide to Training Tough Topics* (New York: AMACOM, 2001), 95.
11. Paramahansa Yogananda, *Man's Eternal Quest*, 114 (see chap. 3, n. 7).
12. Alan L Pritz, "Spirituality in the Workplace: A New Insight to Business" (Minneapolis: Institute for Management Excellence, 2000), http://www.itstime.com/mar2000.htm.
13. Brian Davies, *The Thought of St. Thomas Aquinas* (New York: Oxford University Press, 1992), 9.
14. John 4:13–14 (KJV).
15. Coleman Barks, *The Essential Rumi* (New York: HarperCollins, 1995), 130.
16. Edward Fitzgerald, trans., *The Rubáiyát of Omar Khayyám* (London: Wordsworth Editions, 1993), 88.
17. Paramahansa Yogananda, *Wine of the Mystic: The Rubaiyat of Omar Khayyam—A Spiritual Interpretation* (Los Angeles: Self-Realization Fellowship, 1994), 189.

Index

INDEX

B

Backward Spinal Stretch, 150–51

Balancing Breath, 167

bathing, 125–26

battle, 111, 119

behavior

    guidelines for right, 71–118

    toxic, 40–41

belief on a name, 59–60

bells, 107

Benedictine monks, 154

Benson, Herbert, 101–2, 194

Bhagavad Gita

    on presence of God, 97

    on rarity of illumination, 176

    on seeking divine union, 51

    on surrender, 81

    symbolism in, 111

    on universe as projected

        thought, 49

Bible

    on belief in master, 57–58

    on centered energy, 85

    on creation, 49

    on prayer, 192

    on spiritual realization

        within, 175

Bliss, 203

blood pressure, 102

body. *See* physical body

body awareness, 100–101

Body Divine, 49

brain, 155

breathing

    energy exchange and, 185–86

    exercises, 144, 160–69

    life force and, 160–69

Breath of Light, 164–67

Broken Trail (television series), 1

Buddha

    on desire, 24

    as enlightened teacher, 4, 29–30

    Middle Way of, 114

Buddha nature, 200

Buddhism, 29

C

caduceus, 158–59

calmness, 67–68

Campbell, Joseph, 214

candles, 107, 215

causal (ideational) body, 19, 21, 169

celibacy, 89, 129

Centering Breath, 161–62

chakras

    as archetypal aspects of creation, 155

    attributes of, 205

    energy and, 89

    in palms, 140–41

    as rungs of Jacob's ladder, 159

    sound vibrations of, 203

    system of, 64, 154–58

    in world religions, 121

champions, 119

channels of energy, 158–59

chanting, 95

guru. *See* teachers
guru-disciple relationship, 30–32, 59

H
happiness, 2
Haridas, Sadhu, 187
harmony, 75
hatha yoga, 102, 106, 145, 169
healing
   breathing and, 164
   hands in, 140–41
   Hermes and, 158–59
   by Jesus, 59–60
   nervous system and, 126
Healing and the Mind (Moyers), 102
Healing Words (Dossey), 192
heart, 94, 184–87
hedonism, 90
Hermes, staff of, 158–59
Hermeticism, 159
heroes, 119
Hip Opener, 152
Holy Spirit/Ghost, 95, 202–3
Holy Trinity, 202–3
Hong Sau Concentration Technique
   mantra in, 187–88
   overview and impact of, 193
   steps of, 188–91
Hum, 201
human beings, nature of, 19–22, 131

I
ida (energy channel), 158–59
ignorance, 26

illusions, 47–48, 50, 89
images of spiritual masters, 215–16
imagination, 119
impurity, 109–10
incense, 107, 215
indecision, 43
Individual Body Part Exercise, 138–39
Inhalation Phase, 165–66
inner life, 177, 233–36
Inner Sound Meditation Technique, 205–8
inner teacher. *See* intuition
intelligence, 14–15
intention, 56, 95
Interior Castle, The (Theresa), 157
internalization
   exercises for, 178–82
   higher perception and, 175, 181
   Vivekananda and, 176–77
intuition
   about teachers, 35
   accessing higher guidance, 56
   exercise to enhance, 57
   as inner teacher, 37–38
Isolated Arm Stretches, 148–49
isolationism, 41–42

J
Jacob's ladder, 159
Jesus
   on being teacher, 29–30
   on delusion, 78
   on devotion, 95

About the Author

For nearly forty years Alan Pritz has trained in and taught Eastern disciplines. A meditation and hatha yoga teacher, Interfaith Minister, spiritual counselor/coach, institutional spirituality consultant, and martial arts instructor, Alan has spent years applying inner sciences to outer realities. As an Interfaith Minister, Reverend Pritz shares Yogananda's teachings on meditation and spirituality as a way to help people of all faiths deepen their relationship with Spirit. In addition to writing *Pocket Guide to Meditation* and *Meditation as a Way of Life*, Alan has produced two related CDs, *Heart Songs: Meditative Chants from the Paramahansa Yogananda Tradition* and *The Art & Science of Meditation*. Alan provides weekly All-Faiths Meditation Services in Minneapolis in addition to various lectures, classes, meditation programs, and spiritual guidance services. For more information about his activities see his website: www. Awake-In-Life.com.

Alan L. Pritz has been authorized to initiate sincere persons in the meditation techniques of the Paramahansa Yogananda tradition, to mindfully represent the gurus of that lineage while doing so, and allow related grace to flow. This was conferred to him by Roy Eugene Davis, a direct disciple of Paramahansa Yogananda who, himself, was authorized by Yogananda to initiate others in the Kriya technique and tradition.

Quest Books

encourages open-minded inquiry into
world religions, philosophy, science, and the arts
in order to understand the wisdom of the ages,
respect the unity of all life, and help people explore
individual spiritual self-transformation.

Its publications are generously supported by
The Kern Foundation,
a trust committed to Theosophical education.

Quest Books is the imprint of
the Theosophical Publishing House,
a division of the Theosophical Society in America.
For information about programs, literature,
on-line study, membership benefits, and international centers,
see www.theosophical.org
or call 800-669-1571 or (outside the U.S.) 630-668-1571.

Related Quest Titles

The Brightened Mind, by Ajahn Sumano Bhikkhu

Concentration: An Approach to Meditation,
by Ernest Wood

Finding the Quiet Mind, by Robert Ellwood

The Meditative Path, by John Cianciosi

A Still Forest Pool, by Jack Kornfield,
with Paul Breiter

To order books or a complete Quest catalog,
call 800-669-9425 or (outside the U.S.) 630-665-0130.